ASSAM : ITS HERITAGE AND CULTURE

ASSAM
Its Heritage and Culture

Chandra Bhushan

Publications

KALPAZ PUBLICATIONS

Delhi-110052

Assam: Its Heritage and Culture

ISBN: 81-7835-352-0

Published in 2011 in India by
Kalpaz Publications
C-30, Satyawati Nagar,
Delhi-110052
E-mail: kalpaz@hotmail.com
Phone : 9212729499

Printed at : Gian Ridhi Offset Printers, Delhi

Contents

Map of Assam

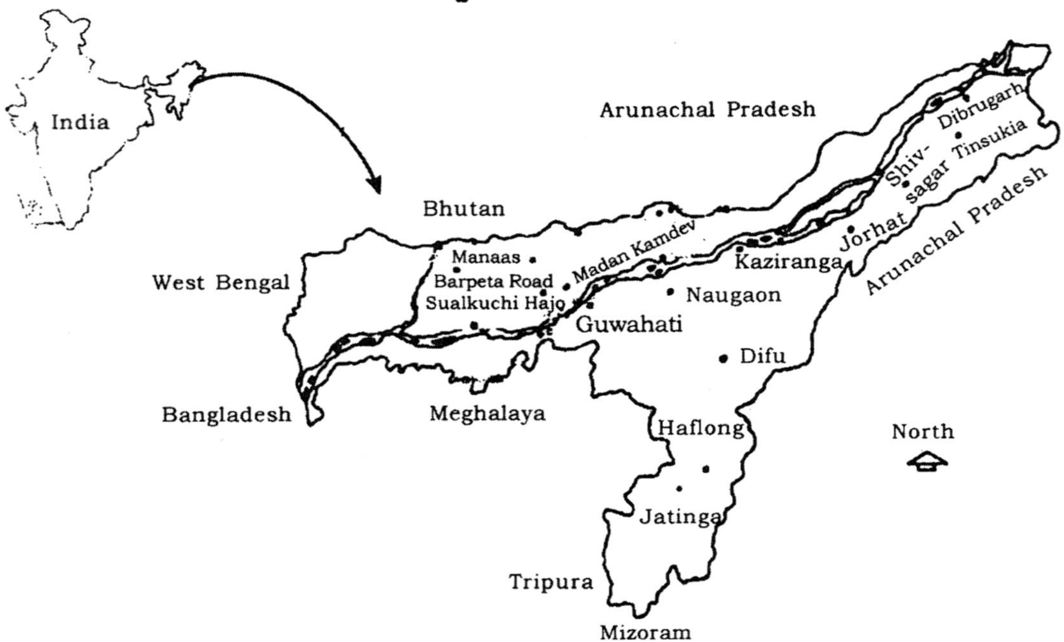
India
Arunachal Pradesh
Bhutan
West Bengal
Bangladesh
Meghalaya
Manaas
Barpeta Road
Sualkuchi Hajo
Madan Kamdev
Guwahati
Naugaon
Kaziranga
Jorhat
Shiv-
sagar
Dibrugarh
Tinsukia
Arunachal Pradesh
Difu
Haflong
Jatinga
Tripura
Mizoram
North

Assam : Familiar, Yet So Strange

ASSAM, famous world over for its tea is a land of jaded mountains, singing waterfalls, merry people and ever-smiling young girls. In the past, Ahom kings infused fresh and varied colours into its art and culture. While in the modern times, Shrimant Shankardev embellished and enriched it with his enchanting poetry and Jyoti Prasad Aggrawal adorned it with artistries of different sorts. Besides the much revered Kamakhya Devi of Guwahati has been a source of attraction to devotees from all over the world.

Assam was also drawn into many clashes while India was a slave country. It was a prey to several diplomatic underhand intrigues and discriminations. Seeds of enimity were sown amongst the tribes of Assam by tempting royal jobs to some, and thus pitting them against each other. Assamese played a significant role in the freedom struggle with supreme fervor and scripted a new chapter of sacrifice and renunciation. However, the state of Assam has perpetually been neglected not only before independence but also, even after it. Successive national government paid little attention to the development and nagging problems of the state; rather, it was largely ignored. Indiscreet religious transformation was the usual practice. Unemployment had upsurged. Spread of literacy among tribes was merely for the namesake. They were not even associated with the main stream of the Nation. Consequently, dissatisfaction gushed over in Assam, paving way to burgeoning violence and conflict all around.

Young journalist Shri Chandra Bhushan set out to write the book 'Assam-VIBGYOR in the Mist'; it was a difficult resolution of course. It was a risky task at the same time, a rather arduous endeavour, to underline the unfamiliar history of Assam, to comprehend the development of the languages and to research upon the various socio-political issues. The good news is that, after years of hard slog, the book is complete and in its present form, has turned out to be a mini encyclopedia about Assam.

Even today, Assam for many, is an ambiguous state, an unknown region. There are very few books available, which document factual information about it. In these circumstances the importance and utility of this book is indubitable. Several movements initiated by the youth, their triumphs and failures get a very candid mention by the author, thereby making it a must read especially for the younger generation.

A round of applauds to Shri Chandra Bhushan for this creation. We firmly believe that this book will be widely read and find a place in most libraries and colleges.

– Jai Prakash Bharti

Mystifying, Inimitable and Distinctive

THANKS to communication revolution that people have started getting familiar, to some extent, with the remote 'seven sister' states (Assam, Mizoram, Meghalaya, Arunachal Pradesh, Nagaland, Tripura and Manipur) in the northeast part of India. People are beginning to take some interest in these states. Unfortunately, the image that has emerged before the rest of India, has been a negative one. The better aspects have taken a back seat. When questioned about the state the common man's unhesitant answer would be that, terrorism, murder & kidnapping are the common phenomenon there. Traders migrated from plain states, face forceful extortion et al.

In fact, elements involved or responsible for creating such an image, or the circumstances involving all these, is a subject of research in itself (See my book- *'Terrorism and Separation in North East India'*).

Here, I aim at bringing forth several untouched issues of Assam. It would not be an overstatement if I were to say that the state is so vibrant in terms of history, culture and religion that no other state in India can match. Epics could be created even from a single aspect of the hills, plateaus, rivers, lakes, various tribes, deep forests, and rare animals that is Assam.

I have a faint memory of why the thought of going to Assam inspired me. Perhaps, It was in the beginning of

80's. Dr. Bhupen Hazarika's film *'Chameli Memsaab'* was being aired on the television. Many aspects of the film, I came to understand much later but what fascinated me the most were the lush green tea gardens, blue Mountains and the natural mystifying beauty of Assam. Since then I had a deep desire to visit Assam- of such a scenic beauty. When I queried my elder sister about the place, I received some really odd remarks like :- "Do you want to go to the state of magic and spells? "Do you know that men are changed into sheeps there".

Didi's statement sounded like a fairy tale to me. After much probing she told that she had seen this in a film on Assam. The episode went into oblivion. My profession in Journalism gave me the opportunity in 1989. I came to know that a Hindi daily had begun its publication from Guwahati; I couldn't resist myself when I got the offer. In spite of my first experience of a long train journey, the curiosity to see the land of magic and spells persisted within me.

I had the first views of tea gardens, mountains, plateaus, rivers, lakes during the train ride itself. When the train stopped at Kamakhya (a small station), I was told that the temple on the Neelanchal Mountains in front was the famous Kamakhya temple. As I bowed in reverence many emotions rose within me, corresponding to the pace of the expeditious Brahmputra that was flowing not far from where I was.

I stayed in Assam for around two years and subsequently kept going back now and then. All the while, various, aspects of Assam I could explore, are presented in the book. I wish to submit again that the book is merely a peep into various dimensions of the state, and should not be considered as any major analysis. In truth, I would be extremely satisfied if I am able to quench an iota of the thirst of the tourists, researchers and inquisitives regarding Assam.

To break the monotony of this book, I have, wherever

possible, taken support of pictures, diagrams etc., that have helped me to slot in most of the living and non living aspects of Assam.

Dr. Bhupen Hazarika has been the source of inspiration for writing this book. What so ever could be written about him would always be less. In the course of writing this book, Chitra Mahant, regional editor of '*Poorvanchal Prahri'* and my friend Satyanand Pathak, journalist Ravi Shankar 'Ravi', Samir Tanti, Reema Sharma, Ravi Kant 'Neeraj', Omkareshwar Pandey, Dinkar Kumar and all those friends have directly or indirectly obliged, by sharing information on Assam. I am extremely grateful to them. At one point of time we had lost the whole manuscript of this book. It was devastating conclusion to my 10 years of hard work. Nevertheless Kalpana, my life partner motivated and inspirited me into rewriting this book on the bedrock of my memories. In the middle of it, came about a pleasant eventuality for me of having to receive Research Scholarship for journalism by K.K. Birla Foundation in 2001. The advantage of this was that I could not only revisit Assam but also could collect my scattered printed material. I also got some fresh input about Assam. I am especially obliged to the Foundation, for granting me the research scholarship for carrying out research on Northeast India and for honouring my writing as well. Besides, if Jai Prakash Bharti, the chief literature and former editor of 'Nandan' had not deeply scrutinised the entire manuscript and also the editing part, the publication of the book would have further delayed. z

At last, thanks to Anamika Singh and Shrawan K. Poddar, who worked hard with me to produce this book.

– Chandra Bhushan

[1] Assam : In the Pages of Ancient History

IN THE pages of ancient history, the position of Assam has remained shrouded in mystery and uncertainty. The ancient story of Assam is exactly like; a bundle of a manuscript that has been drenched in water. On opening the pages of the manuscript, the used ink having come into contact with water is now not legible.

Not even a single script, inscription, or any authentic matter of antiquity is available, on the basis of which any firm conclusion on the state's history could be drawn and a new chapter could be added-up in the pages of history. Today, whatever we can say about the history of ancient Assam, is based on the prevalent puranic stories, folk-tales, some ancient dynastic lineage, remains of a few monuments and broken stupas, which are unearthed by archeologists over a period of time. Other than these, no other authentic basis is available about the ancient history of Assam.

The earliest mention of Assam in the texts of history dates back to the thirteenth century, when a sub caste of Mongol- the Ahoms entered through the Patkai Pass, conquered the region and established their rule in Assam. How was Assam prior to the Ahom era? To establish it, we have to rely only on numerous puranic tales.

There is no certain historical belief even, about the origin of the term -'Assam'. This word is the English version of the Sanskrit term- *'Asam'*, which means unique or incomparable. The Natural prosperity and beauty is rarely found anywhere in the map of the world. That is how the state got its name. However, *'Asam'* being the English version, the name does not have any traces of antiquity. Having established the empire, the wanderers of the world — the British might have forenamed it 'Asam' or Assam after perceiving the incomparable beauty and uniqueness of the region.

According to the historian's perspective, another reasoning, on this subject matter, also seems befitting. When the Ahoms had entered Assam, their magnificent power was perceived and eulogised as – 'came, saw and conquered. Or perhaps, due to the coarse or uneven surface of the land, the state got the name – *A-ssam.*

Above mentioned inferences conclude that the first reason of Assam getting the name can be more than seven hundred years old, as the Ahoms had invaded Assam in thirteenth century. The other inferences seem to have emanated from much recent contemplation, apparently hypothesised after the British rule.

Regardless to whatever had been the ancient history of Assam, It was distinguished as 'Pragjyotishpur' or 'Prachya Praksh Nagri' well' before the Ahoms invaded the state, reorganized its culture, civilization and the natural surroundings and established their dominion in the region. During medieval period, it was known as 'Kamrup'. In the ancient period, in the far off countries, 'Pragjyotishpur' or 'Prachya Prakash Nagari' was famous as the scriptural bench of astrology or astronomy. The adventurous tales of the 'Tantra' bench are frightening. Astrology came as a blessing in disguise for the bench. This is made evident by the Navgrah temple, which exists till date in Guwahati. For centuries, the Navgrah temple had been playing the role of an academic bench for the study of astronomy and astrology. It is described in 'Kalkipurana' that the creator Brahma had created and fixed the constellations first at this place thereupon, the state was named Pragjyotishpur.

More so the region's splendour and prosperity had been compared with the paradise.

Dr. Vanikant Kakati, the renowned historian expresses an altogether different view on the nomenclature - Pragjyotishpur; he believes it to be group of Austro-Asian words such as *pagarjoh* (jo) *tik* (ka-cha) = (c pagar-juh) (jo)-Tic (c-ch) which means a state, surrounded by gigantic mountains. According to Dr. Kakati, 'Prag Jyotish' is a Sanskrit word, which has evolved from diverse Non Aryan languages.

Puranic Stories

The legends have it that the frontiers of Pragjyotishpur included present-day Assam and a major portion of north and east Bengal, which was constituted in the era of Mahabharat during the reins of Narkasur and Bhagdutta. According to Porjitor, student of the 'Puranas', this state expanded up to the Kartova River, which included some portion of the present district of Rangpur of east Bengal. Porjitor's

The emperor of Pragjyotishpur in the battle of Kurukshetra

view gets justified from 'Vishnupurana'. On the eastern front of this state, stood a chain of mountains and passes that stretched up to China. The 'Asurs' were the rulers of this great, widely known and highly acclaimed state.

This belief has been repeatedly mentioned in the epics like –'Mahabharata'. It has it that the state was the kingdom of Non-Aryan king. 'Mahabharata' refers Pragjyotishpur as an empire ruled by Bhagdutta. King Bhagdutta was the son of 'Asur' king Narkasur. In the battle of 'Mahabharata' 'in the battlefield (Kurkshetra) he had fought from the 'Kauravas' side. 'Pragjyotishpur' also finds mention in the 'Harivansh Puran', Vishnupuran, Ramayana and other Purans too. The name also finds a place in the inscriptions of Samundragupt (359 BC). In this inscription found from Allahabad, Kamrup Empire has been referred as the border State of Gupta kingdom.

Thus, the study of ancient literature reveals that this land adorned with huge mountain peaks and inimitable natural beauty, prominent worldwide since ancient times was a non-Aryan regime, which existed in the form of myths and fables since the prehistoric era itself. In 'Mahabharat' Bhagdutta has been referred as a great emperor and warrior. Besides being a great warrior, King Bhagdutta was also a great scholar of Vedas and Vedantas, and therefore was a great expert in Vedic rituals, Vedic ceremonies and religious followings. He could also be accorded as a torchbearer of the coordinated practice of Indo-Mongol culture. This Non Aryan Mongol prince demonstrated amazing bravery and unbending valour during the war in Kurukshetra. During the war, the assemblage of elephants, in his supervision, had led to the transformation of the entire picture of the battlefield. Prince Bhagdutta was high revered in the Kaurava military, due to his expertise in both the fields – warfare and artillery organisation. The defence force of Pragjyotish emperor, as referred in Mahabharat, was a well-organized military of the Kirats and the people of Chinese clans. According to Dr. Suniti Kumar Chatterjee, most likely the whole Mongolian tribe, with Tibetans, Burmese, Chinese and the of other such castes would have been included under a common denomination - 'Kirat' or the denomination was used, especially for the people of Chinese or Chinese-Tibetan clans. Or may be the term –Kirat, was used for the Bhutaneese who were picked up from the mountains and included in Bhagdutta's military.

A lengthy episode in Mahabharata describes about the people in Bhagdutta army with yellow complexion or yellow appearance. Mahabharat mentions that in Bhagdutta's army, there were soldiers with yellow complexion or gold like grandeur. The *'mlecha'* emperor Ghatak of Pragjyotishpur, who was defeated by Narkasur, was illustrated as a golden 'stupa'. Thus, an extensive research and study reveal that despite the widespread expansion and practice of Aryan culture, Mongol civilization was predominantly prevalent in Assam. We are but impelled to conclude that Bhagdutta's following and implementation of Vedic culture implies that the Mongol kingdom too had the Aryan culture flourishing in it. The fact in the given context is also verified from the episode in 'Ramayana' concerning Amrutraj, grandson of Ram and son of Kusha. Amrutraj, most likely the Aryan prince of Madhya Pradesh was believed to have unprecedently contributed towards establishing Pragjyotishpur. This was only because Aryan civilization and system had started making way into the ancient Pragjyotishpur-the fact is substantiated by the context of Ramayana. The ancient Aryan scholars or the military people apparently lacked the inner motivation concerning history. Maybe that is why they did not leave behind any unfailing record, evidential script or historical document on the prevailing conditions, civilization and strifes etc, which could help in unveiling some reliable historical background of Assam.

Renowned archaeologist Dr. Suniti Kumar Chatterjee, while expressing his views regarding Bhagdutta, mentions-Although Bhagdutta has been glorified on the basis of legends and fables, but the same backdrop implies that Bhagdutta, having associated with the Aryan civilization, had played a key role in linking Assam with other parts of India. Around 1000 B.C. enlightened with the light of Aryan civilization, Bhagdutta was the first Mongol king, who was influenced by the impact of knowledge, science and spiritualism (propagator of Brahmanism) predominant in central India. 'Kalki Purana' and 'Yogini Tantra' find the mention of names of many princes titled as 'Danav' or 'Asur'. These princes possibly came into being only after Narkasur, the original pioneer of ancient Pragjyotishpur. According to the parables, Narkasur had extended his territory from river Kartova up-to Brahmaputra valley. After Shri Krishna killed Narak, his son Bhagdutta, ascended the throne. He took part, from the Kaurva's side, in the great battle of Mahabharata in Kurukshetra and while demonstrating grand valour and remarkable war skills, was killed in the hands of Pandavs.

According to Puranas, a devotee of lord Shiva, Banasur, who was the ruler of ancient Shonitpur (now Tejpur), and who challenged Shri Krishna, during the war was a contemporary of Narak. Puranas have it that there was a feeling of hostility between the Shonitpur and Pragjyotipur kingdom that kept augmenting with time. Banasur was a staunch 'Shaiva' (Lord Shiva devotee). He got a magnificent Shiva temple erected in the name of God Shiva near Shonitpur (Tejpur). This temple is known, till date as 'Maha Bhairav' Temple.

The cause of Bana's popularity was his daughter Usha. It is said that a very handsome and desirous man took away Usha's virginity while in her dream. She was charmed by her dream man and developed a longing for him. Chitralekha, a very pedantic and wise friend Usha, having discovered about Usha's plight, sketched pictures of princes of several kingdoms. As she finished making the portrait of Anirudha, Shri Krishna's grandson, Usha bowed her head timidly. Chitralekha reads Usha's mind and with the help of 'Tantra Shastra', retrieves Anirudha from Dwarika to Shonitpur and hands him to Usha. When Bana discovers about Anirudha's stay in Usha's room, he gets him imprisoned. And from here onwards begins the eulogical saga of Bana.

On the other hand, Anirudha's disappearance created a commotion in Dwarka. Shrikrishana anger knew no bounds when he gets the news from Narad concerning Anirudha's whereabouts in Shonitpur and his being in prison. Therewith started the hostility between Dwarka and Shonitpur that finally eventuates after the defeat of Bana. Shrikrishna with his military comes to Shonitpur. A Great War breaks out between the two sides. Lord Shiva Himself comes to save his devotee Bana and challenges Shri Krishna for fight. In the end, Shri Krishna impresses Shiva. And finally, Krishna brings back Anirudha and Usha to Dwarka after defeating and humiliating Bana. The entire episode, including the battle in Shonitpur between Shrikrishna and Bana, Shiva as Bana's savior, battling with Shri Krishna, other than giving the Usha-Anirudha's love story, a religious significance, also enlightens and fills human mind with light of knowledge and spiritual emotions.

Like Usha-Anirudha's story, another Puranic story impels us to accept the ancient existence of Assam. This story is again associated with Shri Krishna. And ascertains the prehistoric connection between Aryavarta and Assam The Kundalpur kingdom (presently- Sadiya) located at the eastern border of this state was ruled by Bhishmak. His daughter Rukmini was married to Shri Krishna. The ruins of Kundalpur are still found near Sadia (around 40 Km from Sadia) on the bank of river Kundils. Sadia came under British rule in 1842. The natives of this state are people from a tribe named 'Mimich'. They claim that Rukmini was the tribal princess of that caste. These tribes, in memory of their defeat in the hands of Shri Krishna, wear a kind of silver ornament on their heads, which is known as 'Kapali'. The story goes like this – Bhishmak had settled the marriage of his daughter with Shishupal, the ruler of Chedi, however Rukmini awed with the stories of Shrikrishna develops a liking for him. She sends a love message to him. Shri Krishna brings in Rukmini to Dwarka on his carriage and tied nuptial knots with her. Eventually Shishupal, with all the hostility in his heart, gets killed in the hands of Shri Krishna.

The mention of these Pauranic stories in the given context is to prove that Aryans were deeply associated with Assam since prehistoric times. However these facts associated with Assam, have been extracted, either from Puranas or mythologies. Following the establishment of Narkasur's regime in Assam, the name Pragjyotishpur was changed to Kamrupa. Before long, Narkasur got the Kamakhya temple constructed followed by the renovation of Kamakhya Shaktipeeth with which, consequently arose the requirement or the motivation of changing the name of the state. On this issue a myth goes like this—Kamdev (Cupid in Greek language) was reduced to ashes, when Lord Shiva opened his third eye. He liberated himself from Shiva's fury and took up his very first physical existence on the soil of Assam. It is the land of Assam, which rendered physical existence to Kamdev, even today the mesmerizing surroundings of which beckons yearnings even in a lifeless body. In the ancient Sanskrit 'Vangmaya', the terms Kamrupa and Pragjyotishpur have been used with equal frequency, especially in the writings of Kalidas. In his scripts, this state has been regarded as the Suzarinty of Suryavanshi emperor Raghu. In *Kalikapurana* and *Yogini tantra*, the name of this state is exclusively cited as Kamarupa. Chinese tourist Huan-Tsang and Muslim historian Al-Barauni have also adopted the use of – 'Kamrupa' or related terms. Dr. Kakati has also concurred the views of these scholars. According to him the state was once, as obvious by the scripts of Chinese traveller and Muslim author, famous as Kamroo or Kamrupa.

Huan-Tsang's journey of Kamrupa

The factual and authentic account of Assam's history commences from 643 AD. The erstwhile history might have held some facts or evidences within itself, however we cannot establish the authenticity of any of those historical incidences, nor can we convincingly assert, anything regarding the history of those times. Instead of being based on history the entire recounting is based upon myths and fables. Nevertheless, the detailed informations regarding Assam obtained after 643 A.D. seems authentic. Around this period, the Chinese traveller Huan sang visited Kamrupa. He did not miss to write about the factual details of the places he visited. The description of Kamarupa finds place in those details. While the Chinese traveller journeyed in Kamarupa, Bhaskar Burman was the emperor of the state. He was a staunch devotee of Shiva and was a blind follower of Shaivism. Huan sang, in his account, had introduced Bhaskar Burman in the history as 'The aristocrat of eastern India'. About Kamarupa, Huan sang wrote - "The frontier of Kamarupa kingdom extends till about 10,000 '*Li*' (approx. 1,700 miles) and that of the capital is around 30 *Li*. Although, the land has slopes but it is very productive. It is being cultivated on a regular basis. People here are involved in the farming of Jackfruit and coconut. These trees are planted very deftly. Dams are erected on rivers or lakes bringing forth the streams, which keep flowing all the time. As regards the climate, he has written that the climate, of the region is tropical and wet. People belonging to this place are simple, honest and modest by nature. They are fair in complexion with a copper or yellow tinge and have short height and flat nose. The language they speak varies from that of the populace of central region of India. These people are aggressive and wild in nature. More so they have sharp minds and are very intelligent.

The aforesaid description of Assam is very significant and concise. These few sentences uncloud the entire picture of the then Assam's rise-fall, success-failure, and development-destruction.

The terms related to *Brahma or Brahmanya Rajdharma* in those times establish the fact that Brahmanism was getting popular among the natives.

As regards the spread of Brahmanism, Huan Sang reports- 'Natives of this place, worshipped God and use to offer sacrifices to gratify their revered God. The state has numerous temples belonging to various tribes. According to an interesting anecdote -Huan sang had first seen emperor Bhaskar Burman, offering prayers in a Shiva Temple. Other than whatever Huan-Tsang wrote about the then emperor, a lot of information has also been collected from inscriptions on copper plates found from Nidhanpur and Dubi area and from the Sanskrit playwright-' Harshcharitam' authored by Banbhatt, which portrays the life story of Harshvardhan, the king of Kannauj.

Darkness engulfs the history of Assam from 10th century to the middle of 12th century. Like the empire of the great king Alexander had disintegrated after his death, It appears as though- after the death of Bhaskar Burman, his empire too collapsed following its division among the incompetent local chief officers and unskilled rulers. But of late, some copper plates, several coins and historical documents have been found that throw light on the history amid these two centuries, and historians have been successful in deciphering some part of the events of the particular time span. Although these copper inscriptions do not provide account of the historical incidences of an era, yet in the historical evaluation, these inscriptions play an important role.

It is true that one could get some details of Kamrupa or Pragjyotishpur in the *Garuda, Matsya, Vayu* and other Puranas, yet they fail to throw adequate light on the data and imprints available of those times. Thus, the historical details of the period of about a thousand years remain in oblivion. This duration stretches from the period of Narak's son, Bhagdutta and his successor, till the period of PushyaBurman. The history of Kamrupa acquires a new form and proceeds towards authenticity during the rein of PushyaBurman. After the death of PushyaBurman, his son Samudra Burman ascended the throne of Kamrupa and ruled till the early part of 4th century A.D. Samudra Burman, during his rein, steered the glory of his dynasty to its unparalleled heights. To be apprised of the comprehensive details of the era, we will have to go through the eulogies of the fifty years of reign of Gupta dynasty's chivalrous ruler Samudra Gupta from 330 – 380 A.D.

Historians are of the opinion that Pralambh Burman was the founder of Burman dynasty. Bal Burman came into being in the sixth generation of Pralabh Burman. In the views of historians, Pralabh Burman fought a war with his predecessor, having defeated him after a ghastly battle and fraudulent designs, slyly married his daughter and became the ruler of Kamrupa.

Princess Amritprabha was the daughter of the emperor of Kamrupa and was born during this period. She was said to be married to Meghvan, the prince of Kashmir. Kalhan, the author of 'Rajtarangini' recounts about the many noteworthy and amazing activities performed in the palace premises of the princess. In his work 'Harshacharitam' Bana

Bhaskar Burman gifts to Huan-Tsang in Pragjyotishpur

Bhatt too, like Kalhan has thrown adequate light on the historical account of the administration of Pushyaburman and his successors. In this volume Murti Burman has been mentioned at many instances. Murti Burman belonged to the sixth generation of Bal Burman, who ruled in the latter part of the fourth century. Following the path of Pandavas, Murti Burman too performed *Rajsuya Yagya.* The rulers of Burman dynasty were the devotees of lord Shiva. The name of their capital was 'Har Roopeshwar' they used to call themselves the emperors of Pragjyotishpur.

Bhaskar Burman, during the reign of whom, Chinese traveller visited Kamrupa, belonged to the fourth generation of aforesaid Murti Burman. He was known as *Shiladitya* of Thaneswar dynasty and was the contemporary of the king of Kannauj.

He ruled from 604 -648 A.D. He was also the contemporary of king Shashank of Gaur dynasty of northwestern Bengal.

There was mutual hostility between Bhaskar Burman and king Shashank of Gaur dynasty. Eventually Bhaskar Burman defeated Gaur king in a battle and occupied a major portion of his kingdom. Bhaskar Burman dominated over a vast area of land that extended till southeast Bengal. The sea route to China was also under Bhaskar Burman. It is obvious that the sea portion of the Bay of Bengal was also within his regime.

According to Dr. Suniti Kumar Chatterjee, -'The state of Assam dominated over a major portion of east Bengal before the regime of Nar Narayan. By the mid of seventh century, Mongols, follower of Hinduism, had established their powerful empire.

History has it that during springtime, Bhaskar Burman, travelled to Kannauj, the capital of Harshavardhana. History also proves that it was during the journey of Kannauj, when Bhaskar Burman met the Chinese tourist Huan sang and invited him to visit Kamrupa.

This dynasty came to an end after the death of Bhaskar

Burman. Around 655 A.D, Shalstambh subjugated the throne of Kamarupa and thus Kamrupa went under the authority of other dynasty. Shalstambh ruled till 675 A.D. Harshadeva or HarshaBurman belonged to the 5th generation of Shalstambh dynasty. Pralambh and his son Harjar of the 5th generation of HarshaBurman were known to be powerful rulers of Kamrupa. In 10th century A.D, the ruler of Pal dynasty took over Shalstambh dynasty. The successors of Pal dynasty claim themselves to be the successors of king Narkasur (founder of Pragjyotishpur). Brahmpal was the first king of Pal dynasty. Following the path of the kings of Magadha, Gaur and Bengal, he titled his dynasty as Pal dynasty. The third prince of this dynasty was Ratnapal. He was very liberal and kind ruler he had immense faith in Hindu religion. While his time in power he constructed several temples. Kamrupa, during his reign, had attained great heights of prosperity and eminence. Also in that period, copper mine was explored and developed in Bhutan. These were used to construct his victory commemorative inscription pillars. He encouraged religion, trade and commerce, besides expanding the Kamrupa border extensively. According to the Nidhanpur stone inscription of Bhaskar Burman- there was an instant and unanticipated expansion of the border of Kamrup kingdom. The empire extended till the entire present day Assam and part of Bengal. The rulers of Pal dynasty had utmost faith in Hindu religion. They took great interest in the spread of Hindu culture and religion.

Pal dynasty disappeared after merging with 'dev' kings. Prithu Dev, the successor of Vaidya Dev, was the ruler of same dynasty. Gazetteer in his-'Rangpur report' has acknowledged Prithudev as a powerful ruler. King Prithudev had constructed giant forts in the capital Kamrupa. A magnificent Shiva temple, constructed by him, exists in Jalpaigudi According to 'Yogini Tantra' he was declared the owner of the land and was named as 'Jalmeshawar'. During his reign, a Muslim chief named Ibn Bakhtiyar, equipped with a band army invaded Kamrupa. King Prithudev, with his unrestrained dynamism, completely aborted the mission. In 1212 A.D, with his valiance he again foiled the attack of Sultan Giyasuddin.

The western part of Assam and a part of eastern Bengal, under the dominance of Kochs had been declared independent state named 'Kamta'. The capital of this state was established in Kamtapur. The most competent of the emperors, who ruled here, was Durlabh Naryan, who ruled till the early 14th century. There is the reference of Durlabh Naryan in 'Pralabh Charit' authored by Hem Sarswati. Sir E.A. Gate's 'History of Assam' also concurs the same fact. The present-day Kamrup, Gopalpara and the Koch Bihar districts came under the regime of Durlabh Naryana, the ruler of Kamta kingdom. Durlabh Naryana came to be known as Kamteshwar and justified his name in having all the royal qualities. Religious leaders, preachers, astrologers, poets and scholars were highly regarded in his kingdom. He patronised and always rewarded renowned Vaishnav poets like Hem Saraswati, Kaviratna Saraswati and Harihar Vipr for their poetic creations.

Following the reign of Indra Naryana of same dynasty, the history of Kamta kingdom became a subject to controversy. There is no suitable and authentic evidence available, to establish the whereabouts of the kingdom. The administration of this place changes again in the later half of 15th century. The Last ruler of Shven dynasty, Neel Dhwaj, annexed the throne of Kamta kingdom. Neelambar was the last ruler of Shven dynasty. During the same period in 1498, king of Bengal, Hussain Shah attacked on Shven Empire. Neelambar fled his capital, after getting badly defeated in the hands of Hussain Shah. Kamta kingdom was disintegrated. The rulers of Bhua dynasty captured and ruled over the different parts of disintegrated Shven dynasty. In the year 1515 Vishwa Singh, a powerful king of Koch dynasty, took over again and established his rule.

Koch Dynasty

The people of Assam strongly believe that Vishwa singh had renovated the Kamakhya shaktipeeth and temple, on the Neelanchal Hills. He established his capital in Koch Bihar. History reveals that Vishwa Singh's reigned from the year 1496 to 1533. After Vishwa singh, his son, Naryan ascended the throne. His real name was Mal Dev. Among the rulers of Koch dynasty, Narnaryana acquired great eminence. He ruled from 1533 to 1584 A.D. During his tenure, art and literature received boundless patronage and thus earned high regard and admiration in the history of Assam. During the tenure of Narnarayana, Vaishnav religion, related culture, contemporary art and literature were much patronized and attained the greatest heights of fame and glory.

Narnaryana, during his period extended his kingdom in all directions. He was a skilled politician, great warrior and expert in organizing the powers. Aforesaid abilities lead him to subjugate Gadganv, the Ahom capital located in east Assam. With the help of his military chief, and Prime Minister Shukldhwaj, who also happened to be his brother, embarked a mission against Ahom colonies. He defeated them and having suppressed them completely liberated Assam of their terror. Aided with the skilful insight of his brother and army chief, he attacked with full vigour on Insha Khan, the emperor of east Bengal'. However, they lost the battle. His brother Shukldhwaj was a courageous warrior and skilled in warfare; he demonstrated such a show of gallantry in the battleground that he was adorned with the title of '*Cheel Rai*' or '*Cheela Rai*'. His name became a household proverb in Assam.

Narnaryana was a brave and skilled soldier. Other than defeating Ahoms, he also won over the Kachhari kings. The rulers of Manipur and Jayantiya use to pay taxes to him and accepted his authority. Akbar, the king of Delhi, was his friend. Akbar had mentioned in his biography that Narnaryana had sent several gifts along with an ambassador to befriend him. Thus, friendship prevailed between the two great rulers who possessed extensive farsightedness and were also the patrons of universal culture. It is clearly mentioned in ' Ain-e-Akbari' that Narnaryana had a huge and powerful army of 1,000 horse riders and 1,00,000 foot soldiers. Except for Brahmpal areas and Ahom ruled eastern Border States, they had unfurled the flag of their victory on an extensive empire including the entire Kamrupa. Their empire extended up-to Kartova River at the western side. And in the southeast side Rangpur and part of Maiman Singh district were also included within their territory. Dr. Suniti Kumar Chaterjee writes – During his period of administration, Narnaryana and his brother Shukldhawaj, who was also his army chief, augmented the prestige of Koch tribe, to its greatest heights. During their rule, the Ahoms were not only defeated but the very options of their re-establishment were terminated. They extended the Koch territory till Arakan, the entire north and east Bengal.

Abul Fajal, in 'Akbarnama' has portrayed the tenure of Narnaryana regime in beautiful words. British traveller, Ralph Fitch has also thrown light especially on how Vaishnav religion, related literature and religious belief flourished and were patronized during his period.. Ralph Fitch has mentioned that majority of Narnaryana subjects were followers of Hindu religion.

During his tenure animal sacrifice and human killing were banned. Having ruled till 50 years Narnarayana died, in 1584. It is already mentioned that Kamakhya temple was constructed during Narnarayana reign. Dr. Suni Kumar Chaterjee says – In comparison to any of the mid era emperors of Assam, Narnaryana contributed immensely towards the study and research of Sanskrit and made extensive efforts to intensify the relationship of Assam with rest of India.

Unfortunately, the kingdom, made out of blood and sweat of Nar naryana and his brother and army chief Shukldhawaj, was divided and destroyed by the successors of their dynasty. In 1613 A. D Parikshit naryana of Koch dynasty established his capital and ruled in Varnagar, situated in Kamrup. Muslims attacked and subjugated the Koch Kingdom. Balitnaryana, Parikshit's brother, with Ahom king Chichenfa's aid, got back his kingdom but he had to accept the authority of the Ahom ruler. It is a fact that the rein of Koch dynasty is recognized as a radiant section in the history of Assam. During the administration of this dynasty, the expansion and development of education, literature and culture was an important achievement.

The tripartite administration prevailed in Assam after the Koch dynasty diminished. Kochs in the west and Ahoms in the east were always involved in mutual conflicts, and Muslim army from outside frequently attacked and dampened their spirits. Not only this, these armies would hamper the growth and peace of the renowned empire.

Ahom Empire

The period of 13th century was quite chaotic in the history of Assam. In this century, history of Assam and the contemporary culture took an unusual turn. People of Tai Ahom tribes of a branch of the ' *Shan*' tribe staying in the Prangbhan or Paran kingdom located on the banks of river Iravati in eastern Burma entered through the pass of Patkai mountain range. There is a story about Ahoms that the prince of ' Shan' dynasty, Chukafa, having been dethroned, had taken refuge in the forest intending to save his life. The fortunate prince found a way through a pass and reached this state along with his group, through that route. As he reached there, he had to struggle with the Chutia and Kachhari tribes who ruled in the northeastern corner. But he succeeded in defeating these tribe, which gave them an opportunity to establish their dominance over a huge area. The history of Ahom's entrance in Assam began, hereafter.

Chutia was a powerful tribe, which ruled in the eastern

part of the valley where Sadia also exist. In 1523, Ahom king Chuhung-Mung attacked on the kingdom of Chutia and succeeded in subjugating their empire. The Chutia Empire became a part of Ahom Empire. And the responsibility of the empire was handed to an Ahom sardar (chief) named 'Sadia-Khova Gohachi'. Having unfurled their own flag on Chutia kingdom, their attention diverted from the hills of north east towards the east. This area was under the administration of Marad and Barahi tribes. Having defeated the Maran king Badancha and Barahi king Yakumcha, they unfurled their flag in the northeast and far east, as well.

The Battle of Kachharis and Ahoms

Kachharis ruled over the lower part of Bharamputra valley. Kachharis ruled also on the banks of river Dhanshri and the land adjoining it. These two kingdoms were quite powerful and served as great obstacles enroute the victory mission of Chukafa and his people. Finally Chukafa and his friends followed the path of pleasing Marad and Barahi to win a control over them and they succeed in this endeavor. They declared their pledge of equality of rights, before the public. They opted for peace route instead of war and following this policy they indulged themselves in the expansion of the boundaries of their empire and were amazingly successful in fulfilling their objective. On the basis of the equality of rights among the people who won and those who were won over, the social and political meetings began. This resulted in the formation of relation between attackers and those who were attacked. Thus the custom of inter-caste and inter-religion marriages started sprouting in the state. This brought about an amazing social change. With the assimilation of the blood of Marad, Barahi and Ahom tribes, a neo swadeshi Ahom tribe came into being. With time the numbers and the power of the attackers coming through Patkai pass increased immensely.

In the 14th century Ahoms fought a battle with Kamtapur

Empire. This incident holds an important position in the history. Kamta Empire had to receive severe defeat in the hands of Ahoms coming from Northeast. And they were forced to take oath to follow peace. After some time, there broke a battle between the people Chutia tribes and Ahoms People of Chutia tribes were also quite brave perseverant and large in number. This battle saw a great loss of men and money from both the sides. Finally, people of Chutia tribe, played foul, and murdered king Chupimafa, who was busy in the celebrations of ceasefire. The murder reignited the war and in 1523 the Chutia tribe was completely destroyed Chuhungmung who succeeded Chupimafa crushed the remaining power of Chutia tribe and incorporated their empire into Ahom empire.

Chuhung mung, who become the ruler after the murder of Chupimafa in 1479, came to be known as 'Dihidia'. Chuhung was a very dynamic and brave ruler. In his period only, the use of explosive weapons started for the first time. They learnt, from Muslim invaders, the method of utilization and control of these weapons. Gradually, they become expert in using tank and explosives. During his tenure itself, along with the expansion of their rule, their culture and civilization too flourished. Keeping in view the social conditions, and the needs of the society they also propagated the systems of social development. The artist were provided with all the facilities to enhance and improve their art, besides other people of the Chutia tribe, who were skilled or expert in any field, were engaged in the development of the empire and even they were provided with required facilities. This era also saw the enhancement of Vaishnav religion and culture.

In 1490 A.D. Ahoms started a struggle with yet another powerful tribe of Kachharis. They fought on the banks of river Dikhao. Ahoms were badly defeated in the hands of Kachharis. This defeat came as a great shock to Ahoms. But they did not take long to muse over their wounds; they reverted back and on the banks of river Dhanshiri, challenged Kachharis for war. Initially, during the battle it seemed that Kachharis would again win over but eventually they were defeated and destroyed completely. Kachhari kings were dethroned and an Ahom king Detsang was made to sit on the throne. But peace did not prevail here for long. In 1536, Kachharis again started a war with Ahoms. As a result of the battle Kachharis imprisoned Detsang and hanged him. Ahoms, agitated by this incident, attacked on Kachharis with full vigour and defeated them. Their capital Dimapur, situated in central Assam was severely plundered.

The fall of Kachhari Empire

Dimapur was established as the capital of Kachharis in 13th century It had extended till north Kachhar. According to a pauranic story, Kachhar Empire was famous by the name of ' Hidimba' a she-devil mentioned in Mahabharta. According to some historians, the term Dimapur is the slang version of Hidimbapur or Hidimbanagar. Thus by the end of thirteenth century, Ahoms had captured over the entire Kachhari kingdom In 1531-36, Chumung Hang or Dihingya had extended the Ahom empire till Dimapur. During the Kachhari period, the empire was the hub of education, art and culture. As regards impact, in 'Kachhari Buranji' edited by Dr. Surya Kumar Bhuyan, it is said – "Kachhari emperor Tamradhawaj Naryana's wife and Surdarp Naryana's mother, queen Chandra Prabha had awarded the royal poet -Bhuvaneshwar Vachaspati, who had translated '*Vrihad Nardiya Kathamrut*' into Assamese language.

Great warrior king Chang mung hang (Dhingya) succeeded in establishing a powerful Ahom empire after defeating Kachharis. He too died in the hands of an assassin in 1539. With his boundless courage he foiled two Muslim invasions after having defeated the Kachharis. After his death, Chuklen mung was anointed the king of the Ahom kingdom. He had ruled from 1539 to 1552 A.D. Chuklemung was the first Ahom emperor, who started the use of coins in Assam.

Mughal Invasion

Assam had always been facing and bravely counteracting Muslim attacks. Several times Muslim invaders, even managed to reach till *Gadganv*-the Ahom capital; nevertheless, they were badly defeated and chased away. Ahoms even, aborted the attack of Muslim chief Turbak, who was eventually killed in the hands of Ahom prince, on the banks of river *Bharlu*. The earliest Muslim attack on Ahom came upon during 13th century. They proceeded to assault on Assam, after having annexed Bengal, in 1205.

In 1627, Muslims carried out a major attack. They did so, in reprisal, after having suffered defeat in the hands of Balit Narayan of Koch dynasty. It was a brutal assault. Besides, it aimed against Kochraj and Ahoms too. This was the 9th Muslim attack on Ahoms. However, even this was foiled. After the failure of this attack a major portion of Koch Empire was included into the Ahom dominion. Ahoms were thus getting more & more powerful and prevailing.

In 1658, the existing Koch king Pran Narayan attacked and defeated the Muslim chief of Gopal para and seized it. However, he was defeated by Jayadhwaj, ruler of the Ahom empire, and had to retreat from the riverside sonkosha. Eventually, the whole of Brahmaputra valley region came under Ahoms.

Ahoms had taken control of Gopalpara. Though it had several times, faced the rage of clashes between Kochs and mughals before, but this time Ahoms had acquired absolute control over it. However, even they could not protract their supremacy. And in 1661, mughals subjugated it once again. With that, Ahoms' dominance on *Gopalpara* came to an end. Finally, in 1765 A.D. it came under the British authority.

In 1661, under the commandership of Meer Jumla, this region witnessed the 11th Mughal attack. Mir Jumla was the *Nawab* of Dhaka. Having defeated Koch king Pran Narayan, he proceeded further, against Ahoms. He had a huge army that included 12,000 horse riders and 30,000 foot soldiers. Besides, he was also equipped with a powerful Navy. Supplemented with such vast band of soldiers, Meer Jumla lead a major attack and gaining an unforeseen success, seized Gadganv- the Ahom capital. But excited, with the roar of victory drum, immersed in the joy of triumph, the mughal army was severely attacked and battered by Ahoms.

In Assam, Ahoms, in their victory maneuvers, received unexpected support from the nature there; the severe monsoon in Assam presented obstruction for Meer Jumla, precisely, in the similar manner as the snowfall of Russia, played a hindrance for Napoleon, while on his attack on Russia. During the reign of Aurangzeb, the Mughal army led by their chief Ramsingh, attacked for the 12th time on Assam. It was a formidably powerful attack. However, Ahom army, led by its chief and a great warrior, Lachit BarPhukan, opposed Mughals with great fervor and dynamism. This battle took place in 1670, at Sharaighat, in which Mughals were severely crushed by Ahoms and their army, too was wholly destroyed. This victory earned, Ahom army Commander, such distinction, that today, his name has become a proverb that lies on the tongue tip of the common folks of Assam. The patriotism, courage and the undaunted vigour of Lachit BarPhukan tinted the history of Assam, with red colour.

Ahoms, not only opposed the invasions of Mughals, but also sat a guard on the plausible incursions from Burma and the allied, far eastern countries. In a nutshell, it would be appropriate to say that Ahoms had structured a strong fortification against the expansion of Mughal empire. The last Muslim attack, on this region, came upon towards the beginning of 1682 under the commandership of Nawab Mansoor Khan. During that period Gadadhar Singh was the existent ruler. He fought a battle with Mughals at Itakhuli. However, it is essential to get acquainted with Gadadhar Singh, who is an integral part of the history of Assam.

The period of Gadadhar Singh

In 1679, under the guidance of one of the chiefs of Guwahati, Bengal Nawab's son, subjugated Guwahati and the city went under Mughal dominance. However, when *BarPhukan* came to know that the people are furious with Buddha Gohain, he took advantage of this situation and unified rest of the officers. He took over the capital and murdered the king. In latter half of 1679, a 14-year-old boy, Chulikafa was made to sit on the throne. The boy belonged to Chamuguria clan. He had become a king at a very early age; therefore he is famous in the history as *"Lara Raja"* (Child King). Subsequently, the king changed over to a Hindu name Ratnadhwaj Singh. In order to be in command of the empire, Laluk Sola BarPhukan married his five-year-old daughter to Ratnadhwaj. Then he conspired with the Queen and got, Buddha Gohain and other officers of the state, murdered. During those times, it was customary among Ahoms, that no handicap prince could become a King. Laluksola Barphukan conspired with the king and began cutting off the organs of the other Princes. However, Gadapani, son of Gobarraja, who was prudent and daring, escaped this conspiracy. Jayamati was Gadapani's wife. To save his life, she sent him towards *Naga* Hills. Jayamati was detained and tortured brutally, whilst questioning with regards to the whereabouts of *Gadapani*. But the devoted wife did not budge a word and succumbed to the torture on 27 March 1680. From then onwards, natives of Assam had been paying their tributes to that amazon, by regarding her as *Sati Jayamạti*. After that Laluk Sola Barphukan also died. He was murdered by the royal employees. On the other hand Gadapani was busy expanding his powers amid the Naga Hills. He came to his brother-in-law Bunder Burfukan place. With his aid, Gadapani dethroned Lara Raja at Gadganv itself; and took over the throne. The same Gadapani, after becoming the king, came to be known as Gadadhar, who battled with Mughals at Itakhuli. Mughal army was defeated in the clash of Itakhuli.

In 1683, Gadadhar suppressed Miris. He ruled till 15 years. He died in 1696. He believed in power worship. He got 'Umanand Devalaya' constructed in 1694. He focused mainly towards rural development and transportation. He had constructed several bridges, roads and lakes.

In every victory mission of Assam, else in the defeat of Mughals or any other assailant, the nature of Assam played a significant role. Assam's Great forests, numerous diseases and epidemics emanating from Assam and the monsoon assisted greatly to stop or chase away the enemy. The ten thousand military sent by Muhammad Shah, lost its way and ended up in those jungles. Thus, the Natural surroundings of Assam offered a unprecedented help in the victory mission of Assam

The Period of Rudra Singh

After Gaddhar, his son Rudra Singh took over as the emperor of Assam. He ruled from 1696 to 1714. Rudra Singh was the elder son of Jayamati. His child hood name was Lai. After his father's death, he changed over his name to Rudra Singh (a Hindu name) and Chukhumfa (an Ahom name) and ascended the throne. Soon, he reverently reinstalled, the Vaishnavs at Manjuli, debased by his father. Since then Manjuli has become the main hub of Vaishnavs. In 1702, he subjugated *Nagas*. In 1707 he sent Sanat Barua and Pani Phukan to attack on Kachhari kingdom and conquered them. The Kachhari king took refuge at Jayantia king Ram Singh and sought his help. Instead of helping, he took Tamradhwaj and his family, into custody. Helplessly they turned towards Ahoms for help from. Rudra Singh sent Bar Baruah and Bar Phukan to attack on Jáyantia kingdom. Bar Baruah attacked on Jayantia and librated Tamradhwaj. He arrested Ram Singh and produced both the kings, in front of Rudra Singh. In 1708, in *Vishwanath Durbaar* he declared Jayantia and Kachhari Kingdom as that of Ahom kingdoms and validated their rulers as his subordinate kings.

Plying to his desire for the expansion of the kingdom, Rudra Singh wanted to attack on Bengal therefore he started to amass military and resources. But suddenly he fell ill in 1714, and died. Amongst the Ahom kings, Rudra Singh proved to be of highest category and the best. He was a great warrior and was highly intellectual. He had made great efforts in the field of social welfare and constructed many ponds and lakes. In memory of his mother Jayamati, he constructed Jai Sagar and Jaidaul. He focused special attention towards education. Dr. Suniti Kumar Chatterjee rightly describes him as 'Shivaji of East India'. He further says-" By God's will, had Shivaji of South and Rudra Singh of Bengal formed a relationship of association; the history of India, today would have been outrightly different. The influence of Rudra Singh's personality was farfetched. Not only Assam but the entire nation should feel proud of Ahom King- Chukhumfa Rudra Singh.

Following the death of Rudra Singh, his son Shiv Singh ascended the throne. 'Chutmafa' was his Ahom name. He was in awe with the Brahmins. After astrologers prophesied his empire's destruction, he entitled his Queen Phuleshwari as 'Bade Raja' and started looking after the royal administration. She was a fine-looking 'Nat' girl. Besotted of her beauty, he had made her his queen. She was not only good-looking but possessed brains too. She had immense faith in power worship. She was enraged when the Vaishnavs opposed *Devi* worship. She persuaded their *mahant* to bow his head in front of the idol of Devi.

Fall of Ahom Empire

Ahoms ruled over Assam from thirteenth century till the middle of nineteenth century. Almost, whole of Brahmaputra valley came under their dominance. The final epoch of Ahom Empire served a battleground of controversy between Shakti and Vaishnav sects. A situation of mutual struggle and subjection arose, involving the two communities. Dark clouds of the downfall began hovering.

More so, the humiliation of Vaishnavs by Queen Phuleshwari, served as fuel to fire. Violent activities commenced there and took a toll. The enduring insurgence encompassed whole of 18th century and ceased finally, after the dominance of Burmese. The autonomy of Assam formerly went in the hands of Burmese and later, to that of British.

Rajeshwar Singh was the successor of Shiv Singh. He was a king without courage. Lakhi Singh was his successor and his tenure of rule was same as that of his father's. He too, was a coward king. His tenure laid a strong foundation of the disintegration of Ahom Empire. The powerful center of the empire collapsed due to the rise of Mobamari branch of Vaishnav band. It left a very bad effect on king's psyche. The king humiliated the Mahant of Mobamaris. At that instance, he left without a word however, the initial revolt of Mobamaris set off, during the month of November in 1769 A.D. On the grounds, when on 15th September 1769, Marana Chief Nahar Khora, Shaikia, and Raghav came to offer elephants to king in the form of revenue, Kirti Chandra Berma accused that 'Elephants are not up to the mark' and got their heads tonsured. Disgraced, both returned to the mahant of Mobamari and there they devised the plan of the revolt. Mahant handed over the responsibility of the rebellion, to his son Bangan. The ambitious brother of king Lakhi (Lakshmi) Singh, who aspired to become a king, was also involved in this revolt. The mutiny broke out in 1769. The king issued orders to arrest Bangan. The rebels executed the security men, who went in pursuit. The king sent his military. The military and the insurgents battled on the banks of Dibru River wherein the Ahom army lost. The king fled to Guwahati. Several officers were arrested and many amongst them were executed.

Subsequently, the revolt was somehow suppressed by killing Naher, Maran, Mahant, Ramakant and other rebels by hook or crook and Lakhi Singh was enthroned again. After the Mobamaria revolt, Deo Dhai Pandit convinced him that he went through so much of trouble after quitting to follow Ahom's principles. The king accepted the pundit's stance yet the influence of Hindu religion kept on increasing on him. Lakhi Singh had conceived several development plans. Some he could accomplish, and some were left half way through, when he died in 1780.

After he died, some leaders of the empire crowned his son Gauri Singh the king. As soon as he ascended the throne the king started getting the organs pierced, of all those who were suitable to be the Kings. Mobamari revolt resurfaced due to his tortures. Suddenly one night, the insurgents entered the city of Gadganv and slaughtered countless people. They set Shinghri house on fire. Some how the king managed to flee. However, the rebels were once again chased away with the help of Ghanshyam Buddhagohain's military. King returned back to his capital and on Barbarua's recommendation, executed thousands of Mobamaris. On the other hand, Mobamaris declared the onset of mutiny, at the northern side of Brahmaputra. The king's brutality only made the matters worse; the insurgence fully engrossed itself in destroying the royal administration. Mobamaris plundered men and material, they burnt and destroyed many villages. The king Gaurinath failed to curb this revolt. He appealed to the British Government, for help. In 1792, East India Company sent Capt. Wales as his aid. This mission concluded with a treaty between Gaurinath and Captain Wales. According to Sir E.A. Gait. "Gaurinath Singh was the most incompetent, bloodthirsty, denigrated, coward of all Ahom Kings". In 1795 Gaurinath died. After him, Kamleshwar Singh became the king, who ruled till the year 1811. He was a descendant of Gadadhar and his original name was Kinaram. Having ascended the throne, he rechristened himself a Hindu name Kamleshwar Singh and an Ahom name Chuklifan. He ruled for about fifteen years. He succeeded in sustaining his reputation, by running a regimented empire. Following the death of the king, Budhagohai, the whole soul of the empire, made Chandra Kant, the king's brother, sit on the throne. Administration of the empire had weakened and disintegrated because of religious and political uprisings.

Attack of Burmese

It was during the reign of Chandra Kant that, on the invitation of Badan Phukan, who had been banished by Buddhagohai, a band of 8000 Burmese soldiers were sent to Assam for his help to fight against the emperor. Purnanand Gohain sent the military against them and a great battle broke out between the two. Ahoms lost the battle. At the same time Purnanand Buddha Gohain died. His son Ruchinatha took over as the Buddha Gohain. He again sent military against Burmese but they too were defeated. Burmese enthroned Badan Bar Phukan on the post of Buddhagohai; they took away a lot of riches, gold, pearls and stones and also took along Hemo Kumari for Burmese king. King Chandrakant was now a king just for the name's sake. He became a puppet in the hands of Badan Bar Phukan. Due to this, Royal mother was also unhappy with Budan Burphukan. Everyone began to despise Badan Burphukan. In 1818, a soldier named Roop Singh murdered him. Chandrakant was restrained from becoming the king. Instead, with Budhagohains' or Ahom prime minister's wise efforts, Purander Singh was made the king.

But once again Budhagohai had to face trouble. Dethroned King Chandrakant sent a message to Burmese King for clandestine murder of Badan Burphukan. The Burmese king at once sent a band of military. Purander Singh fled and Chandrakant again became the king. But he too, was a king for the name's sake. The power was virtually in the Burmese hands. From the period 1819 to 1824, Burmese ruled predominantly. Following the treaty of 1826, between Burmese and British, the Royal administration went in the hands of the British.

In the history, the period of the fall of Ahom Empire is considered as dark era. This was a time when, the entire state, from one end to another was bleeding of civil wars and lawlessness. Terror engulfed the entire valley. Frequent Burmese attacks and brutal massacres had created heaps of skeletons. Burmese military commander, Mingi Maha Bandula's barbaric killings had reddened even the already blood soaked saga of Assam. In front of his genocide, even Ghenghis Khan's barbarity seemed diminutive.

Burmese attacks, natural and spiritual calamities, epidemics and civil wars had left a poor impact on the population and inhabitants of this place. All said and done, despite foreign invasions, the way, Ahoms preserved Indian Culture, empowered and developed Viashnav religion, protected Hindu customs and tied them with the cord of unity, the way they looked after, took care and conserved it; one wouldn't feel hesitant to acknowledge it as an admirable step in the Indian history. It is natural to feel indebted towards the accomplishments of the Ahoms.

Ahom Administration

Ahom administration was neither complicated nor was it tied down with any constitutional chord, which would make it, incomprehensible. Rather, the royal system was very simple. On the top level, the head of the empire used to be the king. He would be the official of the grand, extensive and universal empire. He was not supposed to go wrong or be unjust. To be counselled on every issue of the state, the king had three persons famous as Gohains (ministers). They were known as 'Mantri Parishad' (council of Ministers). These Gohains or ministers had extensive rights and were considered three pillars of the state -Be it, external, internal, war or peace related etc; on any of such issues king would seek their advice. Generally State's policy related plans were formulated by the 'Gohains' or ministers and the king would then implement these, through his universal rights. On the issue of hereditary rights, it was a rule that after the father the son could only inherit his throne. This ruling though, was followed strictly in the initial stage of Ahom rule. However, later on, mutual rivalries led to its violation.

The king was highly revered and regarded as an individual; and in every stately issue he used to be addressed with such remarkable names as '*Swarag dev*' (God of Paradise) or '*Swarg Prabhu'* There was a condition that a prince could only become a king if he had no signs of some physical injury. According to Dr. Suryakumar Bhuya- " Ahom regime was a kind of aristocratic administrative system. There was a law to select the king from amongst *Dihingia, Charingia, Tunkhungia, Namrupriya, Chamuguria* and *Parvatia* families. The coronation ceremony of the king was celebrated with great fanfare. It was merely a demonstration of affluence and poise of the rank. Ministers or *gohains* belonged to superior families. Bargohain, Budd*hagohain* and *varpatr gohains*-these *gohains* or ministers enjoyed the right to have a set number of servants for their personal use. Bar Baruah and Barphukan were also amongst the elite families of the state. Royal representatives for district administrations were often selected from these families. The other ranks of the state were determined on the basis of their efficiency and standing. And the importance and social level of that position was also defined.

Ahoms constituted a navy also. The officer who supervised this armed organization was known as *Pani Phukan* or *Nau Chalia Phukan* meaning- royal chief of navy. A Judge was known either as '*Nyaya Sodha Phukan'* or an official of justice. Explosives factory, security of the state fort, and Queen's jobs had various offices. Other than the defence or military ranks, there existed some civil ranks as well. They too enjoyed many rights and precincts.

People of '*Katkikul*' were appointed for diplomatic purposes. During the time of war or peace, people from these families were appointed to reinforce the diplomatic relations with foreign nations or regional conventions. For instance, Ratnakandli and Arjundas who belonged to these families; King Rudra Singh sent them with a confidential letter to king Ratna Manikya of Tripura.

Like the ancient Roman or Greek Courts, the judges or elite people had name-bearing writers as their subordinates. The Dallai people of Assam were usually astrologers. They used to foretell happenings. '*Paiks*' would serve their lords. In those times, purohitism, which enjoyed the reverence and recognition of the masses, was also a part and parcel of elitist government system. They did not indulge in any manual task related to state affairs. They were also allocated with land or *Jamindaris*. They were highly esteemed. In the event of necessity, anyone from the age group of 15 to 50 years had to go for state service The Elite were often guided by purohits. They were of high social standing and enjoyed and many amenities. Besides, a large segment of the general public of the state was known as *Kari, Teerandaj, Paiya* or foot soldier.

A security officer was appointed with *Paiyas* or foot soldiers, who was assigned with a special troop under him. A *Bara* had 20 *Paiks* under him. A *shaikia* one hundred, Hazarika had one thousand, Rajleva had three thousand and a Phukan had six thousand soldiers under his control. The whole of this security system united within strict administration. Paiks received three acres of land, in lieu of their services. This land was exempted from revenue. In addition, they were given land for house or garden, in lieu of that, they were supposed to pay just one rupee to the royal treasury, as individual tax or house tax. Elites or officials possessed their own *Jamindaris*.

The judicial system of Ahom government was based on a strong foundation. The three *Gohains* or ministers were chief judicial officers. They not only held the responsibility of state administration but also looked after law and commerce. The penal code of conduct was complete in itself. Various excruciating sentences or death sentence were the forte of general law and order. The shape of their administration was like a imaginary pyramid. On the top was a king, then the ministry and then Paik and Karis. Chain of command and expertise were the watchwords. The security of this system was done with utmost will and efficiency that was mandatory for the whole system. Sword was the chain of this system and death sentence was the justice. According to Dr Suniti kumar Chatterjee "Prior to it, such a practical, extensive and efficient system had not been witnessed neither in Asam nor in the whole of India The army unit and administrative system of Assam is the gift of Ahoms. Not only in Assam, rather in the entire India. Ahom's were so powerful that the name of the empire, which they established became associated with them in the form of a nation.

[2]
British Administration System and Contribution of Assam in Freedom Movement

EVEN after the Burmese drove the British forces away from the Brahmaputra Valley in 1826, there was no visible improvement in the condition of Assam. Burmese invasion had made life extremely miserable. The Burmese military had weakened the state through economic and environmental exploitation. More than half of Assam's population had fled from the state and majority of those who remained took excuse of the prevailing anarchy and joined ranks of anti-social elements. The absence of an able ruler resulted in an undisciplined and unrestrained populace. It was during this completely spoilt and pathetic stage of affairs that David Scott, a representative of East India Company took the reins of Assam.

After taking over the administration, David Scott, Gambhir Singh was made the King of Manipur. Jayantia's King was reinstated on the throne. According to the treaty of 6 March 1824, Govind Singh was carinated as the king of Kachhar, only after making a deal to pay Rs 10, 000 annually to the company, he acquired the rights of the throne. Other than the internal matters of the state, he was totally under the authority of British administration.

In the Brahmaputra valley, English representative David Scot at first, paid special attention towards the kingdoms of Chinfau, Khanti, Matak and others. Before getting appointed as the ruler of Ahom and Northern Assam, he had been the commissioner of the district of Rangpur and Govalpara but now he had to take over the responsibility of the administration of an extensive and a distraught area. To manage such an expansive state but dilapidated and ruined in the hands of Burmese invasions, seemed an Herculian task to him. Having sensed his dilemma, company's government appointed Colonel Kapoor, Captain Newville, Capt Adam White and other officers for his aid. With the help Assam Light Infantry, Captain Newville overpowered the people of Chinfau and subjugated the eastern region of Assam and established peace in that area. The next step of David was to make a deal with Matak Empire of upper Assam. Matak kingdom used to pay taxes to Ahoms. Ahom kings used to address Matak ruler as *'Bar Senapati'*. In 1826, British representative entered into a deal with Matak Empire and took $2/3^{rd}$ of the Paiks under his possession. But this deal did not last longer. Consequently, English demanded 12,000 Rupees in lieu of the *paiks*. The Matak king, who used to pay tax to Ahom king, put this matter across to him. On Ahom king's stance, this amount was reduced to 10,000 Rupees. In 1835, English again entered into a treaty with Matak State under which, in addition to the payment of tax company's other demands were also fulfilled. Same way, the Khanti state was given the responsibility to bear the expenses of only 10 British soldiers posted for the security of the border.

From Chimphau also, after having recognized it as village, company drew a lot of benefits. The first was, the troop of 80 soldiers had to promise their support to British administration. Secondly British started getting regular reports of Burmese transmigrations through Patkai pass. In this way Matak, Khanti and Chinfau states were made the agency regions.

Now David diverted his attention towards the valley of Brahmaputra. British had entered the Brahmaputra valley with a prior intention to chase away the Burmese military from the valley but they did not go back even after chasing the Burmese away. Instead, embarked upon the expansion of the Company's empire. According to Yandabu Treaty, Assam was declared under British possession. However, the British had already captured the valley of Brahmaputra, a year before having signed the treaty. Company government had divided Assam into two parts- Upper and Lower Assam.

With the support of his aids, David Scott besides solving Assam's problems had also organized a system for taxation. The responsibility of Judiciary was given to Panchayat. The system of hearing of the judicial cases was safe in the Commissioner hands.

Dissatisfaction among a group of peoples in Assam started increasing due to the imperialistic approach of British. In the beginning, the efforts were made for the freedom from the shackles of dependence. Gamdhar Konwar made the first attempt in this field and declared himself the king. Kaandura Deka Phukan, Dharmdhar Mantri, Piyali alias Dhananjay, Bhaga Bargohain and his son Harnath gave their full support to Gamdhar Konwar in his mission. Lt Buther suppressed this rebellion. Commissioner of Assam sentenced Konwar to 7 years of imprisonment. His other associates were also given rigorous punishments. Harnath was released. And with the skills of his intellect, he also got his associates released from the jail.

After this, many other people too conspired against the British. Piyali or Pobali Bar Phukan, son of Badan Chandra Bar Phukan, was the leader of these rebellion activities. On 25 March 1830, they had planned to, free Assam by exploding the Rangpur military area, and by killing the British military and the Britishers, who were posted there. The rebels formed a good network with the other states regarding this plan and then set the Rangpur explosives house on fire. But since the British soldiers were vigilant enough, the rebels could not succeed and they were caught.

They went under trial in the court of Newwill. There was one Bargohain and one Bar Baruah of Assam in the court. Court ordered death sentence to Piyali Bar Phukan,

Jeu Ram, Dulia Baruah, Roopchand Konwar, Deoram Dehidia, Baum Chinfau and Harnath. After the appeal in the court of commissioner in Cherapunji, he convicted Piyali Bar Phukan and Jeo Ram Dulia Baruah as the conspirators and sustained their death sentence after declaring them the rebels. Others were expatriated for 14 years and their property was confiscated.

Even after so much, the fire of discontentment did not blow out and the spark would reignite on any pretext. In comparison to the people of other states of India the Assamese seem to be more sentimental for Independence. After Piyali Barphukan, Jeo Ramdulia Barua were hanged and others were sent in exile, Dhatua Gohain and his son Gadadhar contacted Burmese king, to conspire, to cast out British from Assam. But this effort too, went in vein.

Such awakenings for Independence explain that Assamese did not easily or willingly accept the British rule. David Scott was an intelligent administrator. He repeatedly adviced the Company officers to make the King from amongst a native Prince of Assam, or else they might have to face obstacles in the administration there. The company accepted the advice and the British representative decided to make Purinder Singh the King. In 1833, a treaty was signed in which Purinder Singh was made the King of a part of Assam, barring Sadia and Matak states. In lieu of this, Purinder Singh had to pay a sum of Rs. 50,000 annually, as tax. British handed the responsibility of Assam to Purinder Singh but kept their direct contact with Sadia and Matak states. An army camp was established at Sadia, and a political agent was appointed there. A new capital was instituted. Arrangements of some soldiers were made in Jorhat for security purpose and the rest of the army camp was transferred to Vishwanath.

In 1831, Robertson became the Commissioner. In 1834, General Jane Kins became the commissioner of Assam. During his tenure Assam was divided into three districts-Gowalpara, Kamrup and Darang. The responsibility of the administration of Assam at that time was with commissioner, who acted as an agent of the Governor General of Calcutta.

After having established absolute establishment of British dominion over whole of Brahmaputra valley, David Scott tried to create some link between Surma valley and Brahmaputra Valley through Khasi Mountain. And after he decided to construct the route; he started the construction of the route from Rani to Nakhon. But Khasi *Siyem* (King), Tirot Singh and his followers, suddenly attacked and killed two British officers and sixty Indian soldiers at Nakhon. However Tirot Singh had to surrender to British. After the surrender of Tirot Singh, Khasi State also went under British possession.

Till 1830, Kachhar and Jayantia State stood away from the British reach. But after the treaty of 1830, Govind Chandra was made the king of Kachhar. After the death of Govind Chandra in 1830, the rebels demanded a separate Kachhar state. But the British did not agree. And after declaring a pension of Rs 50 to the army chief Tularam, Kachhar was completely taken within British possession. On March 15th 1855, Captain Lister carried out a military proceeding and included Jayantia under British rule.

Thus the intentions of British who came as savior to drive out Burmese from Assam became obvious to the people of Assam only when David Scott assigned pension to two of the emperors of the east, King Chandrakant Singh and Yogeshwar Singh and consequently established the Company's rule over upper and lower Assam. And the responsibility of the administration of Assam was given to Purinder Singh in lieu of Rs. 50,000 annually. Purinder Singh made Jorhat his capital and started conducting the administration. At the time when Purinder Singh took over the administration, Assam was as it is going through great trouble. Purinder Singh only contributed in making the matters worse. He did not pursue the route of development of Assam; rather he followed the path of its destruction. It was a heinous task to extort tax from the general public who was already starving due to Burmese Attack. Under the influence of British Feudal system, the king ended the traditional facilities and Prima facie administrative system. With this the influence of Purinder Singh also came to an end. The British were on a look out for an appropriate opportunity and as Purinder Singh fell off from the eyes of his subjects, he was given pension and removed from the state in 1839, under a declaration. And the British power was entirely established in Assam. After that upper Assam (1838), Khamati state (1835) came under British rule. Sadia Khova Gohain wanted to keep Sadia, an Independent region. British terminated him and even defunct that rank. British took over Khamati state without taking any tax. But the people of Sadia became suspicious of the intentions of the British policies. In January 1839, the English political agent of Sadia was murdered. British troop immediately reached there to reprimand the people of Sadia. Many people were arrested and British rule was established. In 1839, on pretext of mentioning the over time limit of the treaty, the British requested to leave a part of Matak for them besides they also demanded more tax stating that the current taxes were less.

When Majhla Gohain turned down the British proposal, the British representatives subjugated whole of Matak Kingdom. And in 1842, British established Dibrugarh as their capital.

In 1840, after army chief Tularam's death, The British representative took advantage of the controversy for the kingdom between the twin sons of Tularams son, and he took their state under his possession and included this new territory into the New Kachhar region.

Ahoms had never had a battle with the people of Naga tribes, who were spread from Manipur Hill till Patkai pass. They always followed the policy of harmony and goodwill with them. Initially British too followed the same policy but later on they followed the policy of "Divide and rule".

General Jenkins and Pumburten crossed the cumbersome hill route of Manipur to reach Naigaon. They compiled and handed over to the government, a lot of information regarding Nagas. Government instigated for battle, the Angai Nagas, located in the state of army chief Tularam and Manipur. Subsequently, from 1835 to 51, total 10 battles were fought against Nagas. And eventually, British army camps were established on the British border for the suppression of Nagas. The British subjugated Angami State of the highland of Daiyang after a severe attack in 1866. They started their administration after Kohima was made the capital in 1878.

On April 1,1898, Lusai Mountain was under Bengal. Chief commissioner of Assam carried upon the administration of the rest of the region through a political agent. This system was brought to an end and the whole Lusai Mountain went under the chief commissioner. And, the chief commissioner started looking after the administration through a Police superintendent. To run an efficient government, he established Shillong as his capital in 1864.

The Contribution of Assam during Freedom Movement

British East India Company came to India merely as a trade company. But it is a miracle of destiny that it went on to become the be all and end all for India. Aided with treachery, deceit, and power play, Britishers subjugated all the states one by one, and one day, established their dominance in the entire country. Which resulted in a severe blow to the economic, political and social system of India. The Indian culture was severely affected. When the intentions of British began unveiling, the suffering of public metamorphosed into resentment. Thereafter, few self-respecting fanatical patriots resolved to revolt against the political power. They were determined to throw them out of India. The dissatisfaction against British among the Indian public started taking a dreadful form. In 1857, the same dissatisfaction, blasted like explosives. Although it is known as military mutiny in history but in fact it wasn't actually a military mutiny. It was the first trumpet sound of Indian freedom struggle. In 1857, Indian soldiers of the North India raised the voice of the revolt against the British and warned them-" Britishers, Quit India".

Assam was not untouched by the revolt. There was also an extensive grounding going on for the same but the British officers were prudent enough. The fire of the mutiny was extinguished. All the efforts of the soldiers failed. Many, facing the atrocity of the British, received death sentence. They were Maniram Dewan, Piyali Baruah. And Madhu Malik, Trinayan, Kamla Baruah, Duliram Baruah, Marangi Khova Siohai, Mayaram Nayar Bahadur Musia were sent in exile.

The soldiers of First Light Infantry Balvant Singh, Ramtahal Singh, and Kriparam were expatriated. In Golaghat, majority of the defence soldiers were terminated. The most important issue was that Kandarpeshwar Singh; Grandson of King Purinder Singh was kept in custody, initially in the jail of Alipur and then in Vardhaman. Where in Kandarpeshwar Singh, died in 1880.

There were many reasons causing the difference in duration of Assamese revolt. The main was Yandabu treaty of Assam on the basis of which English succeeded in establishing their empire. Although the state became free from the brutalities of the Burmese, but it severely got entangled in British hold. Ahom Empire and its officials could not free themselves from this hold. British subjugated Assam and destroyed its ancient civilization, culture, traditional customs and the political social economic system. The Feudal administrative policy of the Britishers only infuriated the natives of Assam. Having being deprived of their conventional facilities and royal powers, the former royal officers were on a look out for an opportunity to revolt. English had diplomatically suspended king Purinder Singh and Chandrakant Singh from their respective thrones. After his death, his son Dhankant Singh pleaded to east India company for special obligation. Then his son Kandarpeshwar, too, requested to the company officials but all these pleas went into deaf ears. Many elite people like that of Maniram Diwan's household, were also annoyed with the Britishers. In 1839, Maniram Sirestadaar Barua became the *Diwan* of Assam Tea Company of Nazira. Due to differences of opinion with the company officers he quit the job, and joined the tea Gardens of Chenimara in Jorhat. In 1851, Maniram Diwan had a dispute with an officer of the tea Garden. The officer seized all the facilities provided to Maniram Diwan. This weakened the economic condition of Diwan. There were 185 people in his family. Maniram sent a requisition letter on the subject of his economic enhancement writing in all the details of his condition. He also favoured Kandarpeshwar and referring to his economical condition requested to impart some obligation on him as well. The application was presented before the 'Sadar Diwani' of Shivsagar. Mil Sahals was the judge there. He did not pay any attention on this letter. The seeds of doubts germinated in the British minds towards Diwan as he favoured Kandarpeshwar Singh.

On the other hand after Mill rejected his requisition, Diwan Maniram reached Calcutta. He had gone there to speak to the higher company officials with the help of Bengali Mukhtar but he failed. Maniram was now upset with Britishers. He made efforts one again and was once again unsuccessful. This served as a fuel to fire. At the same time, the flame of 1857, revolt lighted in North India. Maniram found manifestation of his intentions by giving his support in the rebellion.

Now Maniram made Calcutta his center, he would collect the information related revolt and send over to Assam. He inspired his supporters and Karpandeshwar for revolt. He also motivated the Indian Soldiers staying in Assam, to revolt. But the officers of Nedhereti and Nakachari Companies complained against Maniram activities to the

British officials. British officials were cautioned. Maniram's plan was, - to ignite the mutiny among Indian sepoys and chase the Britishers out of India. Besides he had planned to make Kandarpeshwar Singh, the ruler and himself Prime minister after re-enstating the empire system. All the Indian sepoys of British army had planned to end Britishers, and they had the support of defiant leaders like Kandpeshwar Singh with them. The first flame ignited at Golaghat. But English were aware of all the clandestine planning. They successfully took control of the situation and the mission was aborted. On 7 September 1857, Kanderpeshwar was arrested and sent to Calcutta. Madhu Mallik, Piyali Barua, Morangi Khova Gohain, Maya ram Najir, Duliram Barua and other loyalists were taken in custody. Diwan Maniram was arrested at the address given on the requisition letter that he had sent to the Britishers. Harnath Daroga and other British sycophants had leaked the information regarding this plan and that is how British could succeed in suppressing this uprising. In 1857, Maniram Diwan, Piyali Barua were sentenced to death, on the offence of conspiring a royal mutiny. The others were sentenced to exile. When a political expert, great economist and the preceptor of the revolt was hanged untimely, the whole nation was stunned. Hallride was the both petitioner and the judge so the rebels were no accorded the facility of self-defence. Even after Kandarpeshwar was proved not guilty British banned his entry in to Assam. In 1858, after Queen Victoria's declaration, Duliram Barua, Bahadur Gaunbuddha, Farmood Ali and others were released. Thus the revolt of 1857, in Assam failed and ceased.

British Administrative System

After Assam went into British possession, the administration of the newly acquired state became an important task. There was a great discussion in the Governor General of Council in Calcutta. According to the contemporary system the special commissioner of Northeast

Rangapur or Gowalpara and Garo hills was appointed as a representative the Governor General of the entire state. Three military officers assisted him. Among these was the Governor of Jorhat and the special commissioner of Ranpur district was appointed as the commissioner of Guwahati for the administration.

In 1839, upper Assam again went under the British dominion and an additional administration of 30 square miles fell upon shoulders of the commissioner. Under these circumstances, commissioner of Assam was directly associated with Governor General Council. The responsibility of the administration of Lakhimpur, Shiv Sagar, Nagaon, Kamrup, Gowalpara and other districts was given to a Principal Assistant. A superintendent was appointed for Kachhar.

Principal Assistant had a major responsibility and he had to perform several duties at the same time. He alone had to bear the responsibility of a Judge, Police Superintendent, education, Post Office and all other departments. Principal assistant and three junior assistants were associated with the defence department. Junior assistants looked after the districts administration in the absence of senior Principal Assistant. On the aforesaid posts only Europeans were appointed. In 1850, for the first time a native of Assam Anand Ram Dhekial Phukan was given the responsibility of a Sub-assistant. He was given a salary of Rs. 250 per month.

In 1861, new official posts were created after changing all the names of the posts under the commissioner. Deputy commissioner was given the name of Judicial Commissioner. Principal Commissioner was known as Deputy Commissioner and Junior assistant was made assistant commissioner. In 1872 the posts of *Sadar Amin* and *Munsif* were removed and these posts were renamed as Deputy judge and additional assistant *Munsif.*

In 1874, the administration of Assam was separated from Bengal and handed over to Chief Commissioner.

District Silhat was also associated with Assam and Shilong was made the capital. In 1905, East Bengal and Assam were

The British administrative system in Assam

unified and under the administration of a Lieutenant Governor, Assam and East Bengal were established. In 1911, this system was brought to an end and the Administration of Assam, again went under chief commiss-ioner. From 1922, till India's Independence Assam was under a

Governor.

According to the Marle Minto reform of 1909, a separate legislative council was established, in 1939. There were 11 elected members, 13 Government elected and 25 nominated members. According to the constitutional amendment of 1935, the legislation in Assam was established with a difference and the number of elected members increased respectively.

Assam had a different judicial system. For which Chief *Sadaramins*, three assistant *Sadaramins*, and 17 *Munsifs* were appointed. Only local residents were appointed for these posts.

Britishers, along with, taking over the administration and implementing due alterations in the system, they also prearranged for the regulation of taxation or land revenue. Each individual had to pay Rs. 3 as tax or land revenue Jamindars (*Khel*) were appointed who extorted taxes from a particular group or community. Some Jamindars or *Khel* together made one *Làt* or *Anchal* (zone), Some zones together made one *Manja* or *Mohal*. Each *Mohal* had a *Maujdar, Kakti, Pyada, Chaudhari, Patgiri* and other such employees Later on Government categorized the land revenue system on the basis of the fertility of the soil after its surveillance.

In 1860, *Diwani* or *Faujdari* system was implemented in Assam. A police department was established for the social security. A defence unit was also established for the security of border regions.

Language controversy was the biggest problem of this place. Initially, during the British rule, Assamese was in use, but later on, due to Bengal's influence, Bangla language came in practice in the offices. The Assamese people considered this language a burden. Anand Randhekilal Phukan ended the preoccupied notion of British and re-established Assamese language in Assam.

At the end of 19th Century British Government strengthened the administrative system of Assam. In 1868, they established a public works department and constructed many bridges, roads and Government offices. The village areas were also developed. Hospitals and Schools were established. Municipalities were established for towns.

As the British took over Assam, the very first step taken by them was the eradication of the existent system implemented by Ahoms. As the company's government took over the administration the lawlessness in Assam definitely reduced but exploitations and atrocities were rising. Being a border state the upheavals of anti-social elements and foreign invaders was a perpetual phenomenon. The Assam's condition therefore went on deteriorating.

Assam was divided into small states under British rule. However they took the credit of uniting it under one flag. But, above and beyond that they had implanted numerous seeds of discord, which are till date sprouting, flowering and blooming. Having a Feudalistic approach, British had encouraged and gave all the convenience to the elites where in the poor section had always been exploited.

The way they spread the communal dissentment among the people, exploited the people economically same way on similar lines managed to get termites in their own roots through political awakening. This political awakening contributed in ousting the British not only from Assam but also from the whole of India. If they had not let the political advancement go on, along with the spread of English education, they would have been still ruling our nation.

Whatever they contributed towards the development of Assam, their intention was not to develop Assam but they intended of their own personal gain. The development of Tea Garden, Road transportation and even the education system was developed in order to flourish Christianity. And they took the utmost advantage of it from business point of view Britishers obtained full benefit. Education system of Assam was also changed. Assamese language, which was being dominated by Bangla, was revived. However, most of the newly established educational institutes worked more towards the upliftment of English language rather than Assamese language. Their missionaries opened new Schools and Colleges. Christian religion flourished profoundly.

Non-Cooperation Movement

Towards the end of 19th Century some enthusiastic young men equipped with English education and morals, resolved to develop national awakening in Assam. These young men, studying in Calcutta, had the sacrosanct feelings of social service in their minds. Educated in English medium, these youths had great regard for their mother tongue. They enlightened the people of Assam regarding the past glory and prosperity of the nation. The renowned authors and poets of 'Jonaki Era', through their pen, gave the message about contemporary flow of incidences to the citizens. Assam did not have any political union, in those times. The first politically inspired union was 'Assam Association'. The organizers of this union were late Manikchand Barual, Ghanshyam Barua, Jagannath Barua and Feznoor Ali. The first seminar was conducted at Dibrugarh in 1903. Prashant, the King of Gauripur, accepted the presidentship of this seminar. It was the only Institute for the expression of political views. Later on, Karmvir Navinchandra Bardolai, nationalist Tarun Ram Phukan, Chandrnath Sharma, Gopinath Bardolai, Rohini Kumar Chaudhary, Vishnuram Medhi, Kuldhar Chaliha, Padmawar Chaliha, Vidyadhar Sharma and the tough lives of other such great heroes of the freedom movement were the yield of this union. The members of this association made the English Government aware of their views pertaining to political questions of the state. This association presented a proposal to the existing Government. They demanded the 1919 Montague Chelmsford Committee to implement the constitutional amendments in Assam as well. During 1920-21, after the formation of Assam state congress committee, the existence of this union disappeared within congress. These enlightened youths, inspired by Swadeshi Movement of Bengal and Home Rule Movement of Chennai and Maharashtra, they were desperate to serve and revive their motherland, and therefore they fully supported these movements.

Consequently, in 1916, Assam Students Union was formed. This association activated consciousness among the young students of Assam and awakened the energies the young students. The responsibility of its presidentship was taken over by- Rasraj Lakshminath Bezbaruah. Amit K. Das, Tyagvir Hem Baruah, Desh Pran Chandradhar Sharma, Rohini K. Hati Baruah, Mahendranath Phukan, Benudhar Sharma, Deveshwar Sharma, Kamaluddin and other such sincere and dedicated young students joined this union.

In the history of the freedom movement of the state, the contribution and cooperation of Assam students union cannot be ignored. The constitutional amendment of Montegyu-Chemsford in 1919 could not appease the freedom fighters. A wave of dissatisfaction, against British suppression policy, spread all over the country. Assam, too was not untouched. The youth of Assam also became desperate to confront the British government.

Non Co-operation Movement in Assam and Mahatma Gandhi

Mahatma Gandhi called upon the whole nation to struggle against the suppression policy of the British administration. In 1920, the storm of Non Co-operation spread throughout the nation. On Gandhiji's call, Karamvir Navinchandra Bardoai, Deshbhakt Tarun Ram Phukan and other loyalists from Assam started the non co-operation movement. Many students boycotted schools and colleges. Lawyers boycotted courts. This movement against British reached to remote villages. Be it Literate or illiterate, one and all participated in this movement. This movement had inspired almost every body. Even the labourers of the tea gardens were also inspired and contributed fully in the movement. The whole of Assam was soaked in the movement.

In 1920, Assam partition from Bengal Congress was an important incident. Later on, Assam Congress Committee gave leadership in the war of independence.

In 1929, Mahatma Gandhi came to Assam for the first time. He visited Guwahati, Tezpur, Jorhat, Shiv Sagar and other places and spread his Non-Violent Non Co-operation Movement. After his departure the national movement intensified in Assam. An amazing political awakening spread through the entire state. Foreign clothes were burnt at several places. Government Schools, Institutes, Trade Centers were boycotted.

At that time 'Congress *Swaraj Dal'* was founded. This group participated in the election conducted by the Britishers. The main leader of Congress Swaraj Dal in Assam was Deshbhakt Tarun Ram fukan. In spite of cruel oppression by Britishers, the movement did not cease in Assam. The Assamese determinately faced the British atrocities. This struggle empowered the Assamese National Congress. The best part of this movement was- Communal Harmony. People of all the religions communities walked hand-in-hand in this struggle against the British rule. There was no one as senior or junior, neither a Hindu nor a Muslim. One basic intention of all was -The revolt against British rule.

In December 1920, the 41st conference of Indian Nation Congress was held at Pandu near Guwahati. Karmvir Navin Chandra Bardolai, Deshbhakt Tarun Ram Phukan, Lokpriya Gopinath Bardolai, Rohini Hati Barua, Vishnuram Medhi, Dr. Bhuvaneshar Barua, Nidhiram Das, Mama Krishnanath Sharma and other such experienced workers contributed to the success of this movement with much zeal and enthusiasm.

In 1930, even the civil disobedience movement was highly successful. In 1930, the participation of women of

Assam in the non co-operation movement was an important incident in the history of Assam. British followed the path of aggressive oppression. The participants of the movement were arrested but the movement could not be arrested.

In 1935, the regional autonomous administration started. Elections were held for Legislative Assemblies. After Congress won with majority, Lokpriya Gopinath Bardolai became the leader of Congress Party. But during election Britishers, with their diplomatic move put across a question mark on the communal harmony. In 1938, In the Government that Sadulla formed, he kept the congress out

Mahatma Gandhi in Assam during Non Co-operation Movement

of it and after his resignation, when Gopinath Bardolai formed the Government he separated the Muslim League from it. Before the onset of Second World War even this government gave resignation. After this incident, several Communal groups were formed in Assam.

In 1936, there started the third and decisive war of independence in Assam. After the Second World War, the Indian struggle for independence came upon with a new dimension amidst the public. On December 6th, 1941, on order of Deputy Commissioner Hamphre of Kamrup, the students of Cotton College, Guwahati were severely beaten up by the police. The public of Assam was stunned by these ruthless beatings of innocent students. This atrocity led to a feeling of resentment amongst the student community of Assam and they too jumped into the freedom struggle.

The Revolution of 1942

Almost at the same time arrived the period of 1942. The August revolution had taken a terrible form. Mahatma Gandhi called for- 'Do and Die.' The public of India as well as Assam took the meaning of it as -'Die'. And all the young, old women, children of entire nation came on the streets with intentions to die. Government's suppression cycle moved speedily. Innocents were shot. British started stuffing their jails with Congress leaders. It had a negative effect. People had come out with an intention to do or die, they went out of control, the whole nation went red with blood. Many social leaders were either shot or hanged. Military shot down Kanaklata, Bhogeshwari, Phukanani, Tilak Deka, Madan Burman, Raota Kachari, Mukund Kakati, Numli Nath, Thagi Ram Sut, Nidhanu and others. Kushal Konwar was hanged.

How long could this bloody cycle go on? It had to end and it ended. On 15 August 1947, British unable to stand Indians dissatisfaction fury and resentment, handed to India every humans birth right- Freedom. British left and departed seven seas away, after leaving marks of discretion, atrocity, deception and characterlessness.

[3]
Geographical Structure

A CLOSE look at the map of India reveals Assam as the first state of India's North Eastern region. The state appears like a quiet bird perched on the crest of a mountain range with the Patkai Mountain range forming the bird's beak. It is the Patkai and Naga mountain range that separates Assam from the mountain ranges of Myanmar (Burma). This Northeastern state of India shares its international borders with China, Bhutan and Bangladesh.

The history of Assam is the amalgamation of the history of Brahmaputra river valley and its vast stretch of striking mountain range. There is an ancient tradition of the mutual compatibility and history of the far spreading river and its valley surrounded by mountains. However, these mountains were separated from the plain areas and were declared 'prohibited area' during the British administrative period. Kachhar district to the South of Assam, and the Lushai hills, both are the heritage of Assam. Khasi, Jyantia hills and Garo mountain range can be compared to the spinal chord in a human body and from both the sides, these are divided into two extensive main valleys. First valley is of Brahmaputra and the second is that of Surma River. The additional land portions of Silhat district of Surma river valley- Pathar Kandi, Ratabadi, Karimganj and Badarpur station were at the time of partition assimilated with East Pakistan which is the present Bangladesh.

In 1832 A.D. Kachhar district was also included into Assam. Lushai hill was included into Assam in 1892. And in 1898, the whole of Eastern border region was included in Assam. All this happened in 1826 after English defeated Ahoms and Independent Assam went under the rule of the British. British gave Assam the legal status of Commissioner ruled state in 1874. Till 1912, it was associated with East Bengal as the state governed by a deputy Governor. After the division of Bengal, from 1912 to 1921, Assam was changed into Commissioner Governed Colony. In 1921 Assam appeared on the map as an Independent Governor ruled separate state.

The pass crossing the Patkai mountain range has a historical eminence for the state. From this point of view, it will not be an overstatement to call it the 'Khyber pass of East'. The reason for this is that- Ahoms; a Mongol sub caste native of Hukvang valley, had passed through the same pass during 13th century and subjugated this state. Since then this state is known as Assam, before that period it was known as *Pragjyotishpur.*

Ahoms won over this place and established their empire. They were successful in bringing in changes in the traditions, civilization, and the appearance of this state.

In the early 19th century, Burmese too used the same Patkai pass during Assam- attacks. History will serve testimony that whenever Assam was attacked, this pass gave way to the invaders. In the 13th century, admission of Thai civilization after the Thai attack is the souvenir of this pass. The Burmese attacks and the subsequent blood bath filling the rivers with red blood streams are the consideration of the same Pass. These attacks have filled up a haunting colour into the Brahmaputra valley and also into the minds of the people. Like Patkai mountain range, Nam Kin mountain range too makes a natural route between India, China and Burma.

Assam is the land of full of natural passes, mountains, dense forests, jungles, huge and terrible pits, inhabited lands and slopes. It presents an attractive and pretty image due to its unique and incomparable natural beauty.

The 2/3rd population of Assam survives on 1/3 of its land area. Till the first decade of 20th century Assam was the land covered with dense forests, huge marshlands and wild bushes. However, today with time there has been a tremendous change in the structure and natural panorama of this part of the world. Forests are being destroyed. But the mountains, hills, rivers are still on their journey with their perpetual course.

Majority of Indians are unacquainted with Assam. The main reason for this probably it being far from the center of the national life. In the map of the world, India enjoys the status of a subcontinent. The mountain valleys have divided the sub continent into four parts and linked the human relations into various sections, caste and communities. Assam is the Far East region of this continent, which being very far and having dense natural surroundings has been, left out from the main national stream. Till few years before, the outsiders knew Assam as the "Land of Magic and Mysteries, Materialism and Wild Tribes". To some extent this thought can be considered true also. Reason being, the mountain ranges here are numerous and insurmountable. There are dense forests, several speeding rivers and clear natural environment. According to soil department, Assam is a state of cold temperate type of climate where nature is generally in a state of tension, especially during springtime and in the rainy season.

The natural splendor of Assam, its unique exquisiteness similar to the eyes of peacock feathers lies in its mountains. In the heart of these hills, rich with its unique beauty, lies Brahmaputra valley. Land area it occupies is less breadth wise and more lengthwise; however the valley enhances twofold, the grandeur of the hills of Assam. The plains of Brahmaputra are surrounded by mountain ranges and are open towards west. Where the soil, brought upon by Brahmaputra and its tributaries, profoundly enhances the fertility of the plain land.

According to Hindu scriptures, the origin of Brahmaputra River is a pilgrimage Brahamkund situated at the eastern border of the state. Its merely a religious belief and nothing in consistent can be concluded about the subject of its origin. This pilgrimage is situated about 50 miles a far on hilly district 'Michim' which was once known as 'Sadia'. A recent research reveals that the Tswallangpo River flowing in Tibet and Brahmaputra River are one and it. The river originates from near the origin point of Satluj and Sindh, in the west of Tibet and the river finally merges near Sadia, into aforesaid Brahmaputra which has also become too vast owing to the confluence of Lohit, Diwang and Dihang. Brahmaputra gets its water supply from the huge water resources coming out of the snowy mountains of Himalayas of the North and the southern hills of Assam. During the rainy season the alacrity of Brahmaputra, embodying a huge water wealth, presents a severe and annihilating scene. It presents a spectacle and describes its vast stretch, exactly like that of the sea view, seen from standing on some island. As far as the fertility and production of the plain area of Brahmaputra valley is concerned, this valley can be compared to that of Nile River in Egypt, which is also known as the "Father of Egypt".

Soaked in a blue tinge of light, the mountain range of Assam embracing the extensive blue sky, present an inimitable scene. During winters this exclusive outlook, which is an uncommon natural gift for Assam that cannot be found in any of countries marked in the world map –this statement is an indubitable fact. These mountain crests amid bluish reflections, strike with the sun rays and dazzle like sapphire as if these were mountains of sapphire These bluish reflected sunrays envelop the plain area with a unexplained, mystical blue wrap. The 'Neelanchal' mountain range where the Kamakhya Temple is situated is so called perhaps, because it appears soaked in the quaint mystical blue tinge. There are several mountain to the south of Brahmaputra as there are to its North. Naga Mikir and Garo Hills are situated to the south of this river where Burma and Tibetan inhabitants exist.

Brahmaputra flowing from the mountain ranges, when seen from the ranges, appears like a ribbon. But actually it is a rapidly flowing river, which is not shallow but is rather very profound. Unlike the slow moving rivers of plain areas, it is not dreary like a python. There are several of its tributaries, many water resources flowing out of the neck of the mountain with thunderous sounds and maintain the continual supply of water into the river. The river also gets its water supply from the snow rocks of the northern Himanchal and the waters of the other mountain range of southeastern side. Suvan Siri, Marali, Varanadi, Manah and Sonkosh are the tributaries of the east. These rivers get supply of water when the ice rocks melt. Dihing, Chiang, Dikhaun, Vangiri and Kalang are the tributaries of South that supply water to Brahmaputra.

'Brahmaputra'- is an Aryan term. Dr. Chatterjee in his book 'Assam : in the History and Civilisation of India' mentions that- Ahoms, after coming here named the river - 'Nam Dao Fi' which means the river of God *Tarak* (Star) Dihing and Lohit rivers flowing to the North East of Assam join Dihang river to create Brahmaputra river and these have transformed into a huge stream. In Sanskrit language this river is also known as 'Lohitya which means red river in Hindi. There is a natural reason for it acquiring the name- 'Lauhitya'. During the rainy season when it flows with a rapid speed, it cuts and assimilates the mountain red soil, as a result the colour of the water turns red. Besides, there is one Pauranic story associated with this name. This story is related to Parshuram and his sins. It is said that Parshuram after killing her mother Renuka, washed the bloodstains in this river to regain sanctification. And could free himself from the malevolence of murder of his mother. However, even this story seems a myth. This is a fact that-Assam has been cited as –'state of red river and blue mountains, and these stand for- *Lauhitya* and *Neelanchal*. The Lauhitya river and Neelanchal mountain (where the Kamakhya Temple and Shakti Peeth are located) are considered as the foundation of Assam's culture. Even the historians have accepted that Neelanchal mountain located amid Lauhitya river and Kamakhya temple has made a great impact on the culture and life style of Assam.

It will not be an exaggeration to compare Brahmaputra with the river Nile. The way the rapid flowing Brahmaputra presents a fearful sight during rainy season; same way, it plays a significant role in enriching the productiveness of the plain areas of the valley. The plain areas of this valley are equally famous for its harvest affluence as it is for its conspicuous natural panorama. During the summer season, on the eastern bank of this valley, the sufficient yield of paddy and production of mustard play a major role in bringing joy in the lives of the people of Assam. The eastern side of this valley is packed with dense forest, numerous wild vegetation and vast stretches of fields.

There are two islands in the valley of Brahmaputra. One of them is larger. It is located at the confluence of Brahmaputra and Suwansiri River. This island is known as -Majuli. The area of this island comprises of fifty square mile. The population of this area is over one lakh. This is the famous pilgrimage of Vaishnav Community. The other island is smaller and is located near Guwahati. It is known as Umanand.

Suvansiri riverside was once renowned as-'*Swarnachurna*' (gold powder) that's why this place was also famous as a trade center. Today, it has thrived, civilized with several Vaishnav colleges, homes for religious leaders and Ashrams.

Umanand Island with its uneven topography is a hilly expanse. The hill is located as an islet in the middle of the river and is the part of the mountain range surrounding it. There is a Shiva temple on top of the hill. During the rainy season, the huge and exuberant waves smash together and generate a roaring sound. These waves melt and tell the tale of the failure of their strikes. Although the spectacle of Umanand, during rainy season seems frightening; nevertheless it is a very fascinating sight. Enriched with their respective natural elegance, both these islands embellish the radiance of Brahmaputra. In addition, there are vast stretches of green fields on the riverside. However, these fields get drowned in water during the rainy season. However, after the dreadful sight of the flood and rain, and when the green grass grows back, these fields regain the shape of finest green fields. Due to the vast stretch of green field people living on the riverside generally involve themselves in animal rearing.

On the other side of Brahmaputra, the sight of well-arranged series of mountains, gratify the eyes. Besides, the giant trees with dense leaves and beetle nut trees; concealed within them, coconut gardens, date palms, the dense cluster of bamboo shoots in the valley, appear to be telling the saga of the natural harvest, health and wealth. The stock of trees having branches laden with green leaves, the straw huts made out of fibrous bamboo shoots and fern shrubs, do not miss to depict the rural life and civilization. The village of Assam is made out of the entire riches that have come as natural blessing. The rural authority exists only in the name-bearing houses and in 'public prayer house'. The population here is in harmony with its natural structure. The areas having favourable natural environment, would comprise dense population where as the population is scant at other places in accordance with circumstances. The average proportion of the population of this place is 200 individuals per square mile.

The history screams out the reason of scanty population. The reason commences from the advent of Ahoms in Assam. After the arrival of Ahoms, this state had invariably been a host to mutual clashes that resulted in the ballet of incessant devastation. Burmese attacked on Assam, thrice, that lead to a great loss of the culture, civilization men and material of this state. The population and the self-obtained prosperity went on diminishing. Not only this, the invaders did destroy men and riches, besides, the natural calamities also contributed wholly towards the destruction of the life here. Natural adversities and medical backwardness that was armed with deadly disease-*Kala-Ajar* obliterated the population and these collaborated to wipe out the population.

The archaeological researches tell that the ruins of the towns enriched with coconut, mango and several natural wealth, have been recently excavated. Those areas today are serving as the rest places for animals. The population of those towns kept decreasing due to natural calamities and frequent epidemics. Some of the population perished due to flood and some succumbed to the jolts of earthquake. This is the reason why the average of the population of Assam is so less.

Assam with its wild animals is a blessing in disguise India. It would be proper to call it an un-systematic or unrestrained zoo. It is an imperishable repository of various categories of animals. Now the Government has taken over the responsibility of the security of these animals. And the wild animals are being conserved very cautiously. There is abundance of elephants in the lower valleys of hilly region. Rhinoceros are also in great numbers in Brahmaputra valley. Kaziranga forest region of Shiva Sagar district is a big refuge for wild animals. Three other forest sanctuaries are- Manas, Sonai-Rupai and Pabhai, wherein wild species are found in abundance. In the present set-up, the total area of reserved forest in Assam is approximately 464 Sq. miles. Wherein Tigers, Cheetahs, bears, wild pigs, wild buffaloes, wild bulls and other wild animals are found. Natives of Assam are expert in elephant hunting Sukumar Bagachi had even written down a book on this art. The book is named *'Hasti Vidya Maharnav'*. The skill of taming the wild elephants was known as Austro-Asian art. The art finds its root here; it developed here and spread to all over India.

Assam is also the imperishable repository of natural vegetation. These prosperity generating expensive herbs are obtained from the mountain basins. Expensive herb, vibrantly coloured flora and rose like multicoloured flowers when bloom on the hills, the splendour of the valley reaches beyond words. The sight sooths the eyes and provides tranquillity and nourishment to heart and mind. Besides being hilly, the land here is sloppy; the pines on it give the appearance of a young girl wearing a veil. The flowers like Balsam, Azalea and vibrant wild roses soak the entire valley into blue, yellow and golden splendour. A flower -*'Kapau'* blooms in of April. It is the favourite among the women folks here; they use to adorn their hair. A flower named 'Bhento' is a kind of parasite plant that germinates on the branch of a plant gets its nutrition from the same tree. The way Assam is enriched with mountain valleys similarly it has plain land as well. The same natural wealth is found in 10,000 feet high mountain ranges and in the Namvar forest of Shivs Sagar district.

Assam is unrivalled in its Timber wealth. It would be appropriate to compare Sal tree with that of Oak tree for the beautiful magnificent timber. On the upper front of Assam, *Sagon*, Ajaar and *Nahar* and other best category trees are found. The timber of these is very expensive and valuable. In Sadia region the Bula trees are found in abundance. They can be termed as Sagon of Assam.

Generally, Assam's climate is wet and humid. But during winters the climate becomes very healthy, cold and favourable. The summers are short termed and they are not as severe as that of other places. Rainy season drowns nearly the whole of Assam in water. This place has the world's highest rainfall; Cherapunji situated on the mountains of Jayantia and Khasi is the world's most humid place. Around 500 inches of rain is recorded here. Thus it would be appropriate to divide the climate of Assam into

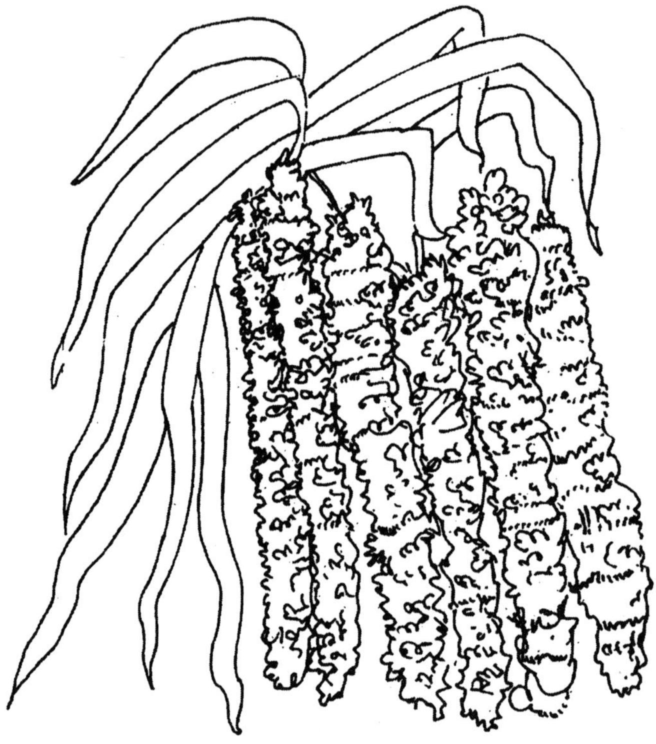

A Blooming Orchid

two seasons – winter and Rainy season. The summers coming between these two seasons are quite normal and not severe and pricking. High-speed storm and tempests are also usual affairs during rainy season. Flood is the natural tradition of this place, arrival of that has become a mandatory rule. The speedy seasonal winds strike the mountain like bombs from a canon gun same way they attack on the plain areas. Incessant rainfall plays a major role in supplying water to the rivers. Swollen with arrogance these do not miss to embrace even the fertile or barren lands on the banks besides damaging the pet animals, crops and the human population. Sometime the entire township gets drowned in the flood.

Assam is also famous for its frequent earthquakes. This state has got the reputation of earthquake-affected region on international level. According to Geologist, Assam is situated in the eastern earthquake limits. The earthquake of 1997 was no less damaging than that of 1950's in which 1540 lives were lost. Most of the causalities were due to mountain slides, river banks slides, earth's contraction and cracks in the earth. The geologists count these two earthquakes amongst the worst five earthquakes in the world history.

Earthquake that came on 15 August 1960 in Assam was the most unforgettable and disastrous earthquake. The spectators provided agonizing details of happenings of the earthquake. It is said the earth that day was vibrating like a furious snake. The hills were moving the way *Sumeru* hills were moving during *Samundra manthan* mentioned in the *Pauranic* tales. The townships were crumbling in front of the eyes. Being a hilly region there was not much loss of men and wealth as otherwise would have been due to the speed of earth's vibrations. Even still, the estimated loss of national wealth was around 5 crores.

To the North of Assam are Himalayan range of mountains, border regions of Bhutan and Tibet, and mountains of Burma to the South. Ahoms after acquiring the state could not resist saying '*Mung dun Chun Kham*'- State of Golden Gardens. A state where yellow flowers of mustard bloom like the golden orchids of daffodils. In winters, the splendorous yellow green paddy fills the valley with yellowish radiance. Having perceived the Natural wealth of Assam these expressions do not sound like an overstatement.

[4]
Social and Economical Structure

TO CALL Assam a museum of variety of caste and tribes would not be an overstatement. History is a witness to immigration of numerous caste and tribes into the region. The Austrians, Dravid, Tibetan-, Burmese, Mongols and Aryans came from many directions and seamlessly blended into one. The Austrians were the first to inhabit the Brahmaputra valley, but after a while, were driven into the hills by invaders. It is said that Khasi and Jayantia living in Meghalaya belonged to the same Austrian community. Subsequently, people of Dravid community-known as 'Kaibarta' or 'Bania' in modern Assam arrived and the Mongols followed them. The people of this community within the Indo-Chinese group came to be known as Tibetan-Burmese family. These people are now known as Kachhari, Dimacha, Rabha, and Lalung Tribes. These tribes inhabit the hills of present day Assam.

Normally, Physical configurations of the hill tribes differ with that of the inhabitants of upper Assam. Assamese have round faces, somewhat flat nose, protruding eyes, high cheekbones and course hairs. Where as inhabitants of upper Assam have yellowish complexion, flat nose, and long hairs. Females have average or short height. In the tribals here the traditional males wear 'Dhoti' and the females wear Blouse and *Mekhla*. However western impact has brought upon a considerable change in the outfits of this place.

There around 23 types of tribals in Assam among which 16 are schedule tribes. The Central Government has received proposals to include many tribals in the above two categories of tribals. Inhabitants of Assam can be divided into two parts,

(1) People inhabiting Brahmaputra and Barak valley and (2) People inhabiting North Kachhar and Karbi Anglong valley. The inhabitants of the valley can further be divided into 4 parts (1) Assamese in Brahmaputra valley and Bengalis in Barak valley. (2) Bodo speaking people (3) Mising (4) People who came from outside. Within the Bodo community are the people of Koch, Kachhari, Lalung (Tiva), Dimacha, Rabha, Mekh, Chutia, Moran and Bodo tribes. Similarly Siachen-Chinese speaking people came during 13th century and they came to be known as Ahoms. The Ahoms community includes the people speaking these languages : Khamiyang, Pakhiyal, Aitonia all, Tai. More so, similarly, Hindu-Nepalese population can be seen in the far hilly regions and city areas. The workers of tea garden also enjoy an importance of their own among the communities here. In the Assamese community, apart from various tribes, people of Bengali, Bihari, Marwari and Sikhs community also exist in Assam. In 1947, after the establishment of East Pakistan (Bangladesh) there came many Hindu refugees but during the Bangladesh war, in 1971-72 both Hindu and Muslim refugees came to Assam and settled here. According to the Historian B N Das-Muslim for the first time came to Assam during 13th century. When Muhammad Bin Bakhtiyar Khilji and his army attacked on Assam. However they were defeated every time. Majority of Muslim from the army were either arrested and most of them did not even desire to budge from there. Gradually, these Muslim married the local Assamese women and mingled with the Assamese society. Presently the Muslims inhabitants occupy mostly the four district of Assam- Dhubri, Gwalpara, Barpeta and Hailakandi. However, according to data of 2001, Marigaon, Nagaon,

Karimganj areas have Muslim majority. Similarly during the First and Second World War when Tea Gardens were established, during that time natives from Bihar, Orissa, Santhal, Uranv and Munda tribals had also come here.

Thus, the present Assamese society is the assimilation of Aryan-Non Aryan, tribal Non-tribal, natives and the outsiders. Inhabitants of plain areas are Hindus in majority and they speak Assamese language. These Hindu Assamese call themselves Aryans, but other communities are Mongols in nature. There is a thin line of difference between tribes and non-tribes. They are quite different with the traditional Hindus in this regard. They do not have communal discrimination. There is a scarcity of crimes and murders relating to Dowry System, untouchability or cruelty towards Harijans. In Assamese communities the people of Brahmin or Vaishnav sect eat fish but generally do not eat flesh. There is one more interesting aspect of Assamese community that here the communal riots between Hindu and Muslim seldom takes place. The Muslim women here do not wear 'Burkas'. The music of Muslim saint Shah Jalal alias *Ajaan Fakir* has special impact on Muslim community. Shah Jalal was the pioneer of the Muslim rehabilitation movement. The contribution of Shankardev towards social welfare cannot be overlooked by the Assamese society. He inspired the Assamese society to be tolerant and reasonable. He started the Neo-*Bhakti* Movement in Assam. Thus, he not only enlightened the social consciousness but he had also been successful in bringing about great changes in the fields of Art, Education, Drama, Music and others. Madhav Dev too propagated this movement. Today Assamese society follows the path laid by Shankardev this is the reason why Assamese Art, Dance and Culture has a distinct identity. Before Shankardev, there was the predominance of *Tantra-Mantra* and this region was even famous for the study of Tantra education. Even today the education of *Tantra-Mantra* flourishes in the areas near Kamakhya Temple.

The impact of Vaishnav sect can be seen in the form of *Satra* (sessions). Shankardev conceived this concept. There are hundreds of session or its branches. They were known for the artistic and cultural activities. Similarly ***Namdhar*** (Prayer houses) exist in each village of Assam. And they are the live examples of the socio- cultural and economic development. These also affect the life here. Some bigger and main sessions are around Barpeta district and at Bardova of Nagaon district (Birthplace of Shankardev) and at other places. But the best quality and unique sessions are there at Majuli in Jorhat district.

In Assam people of Buddhist religion came from Bhutan in North and Myanmar in the East. In fact *'Garib Madhav'* temple at Hajo is such a temple where Hindu and Buddhist both come to pray.

In Assam apart from Assamese, Bangla is also spoken. Besides, Bodo, Karbi, Mising, Rabha and other tribes speak the vernacular of their communities.

In the Bodo area, Bodo language is recognized where as in the barak district Bengali is prevalent. However each community has a language of its own but most of them have accepted Assamese as their own language. In fact, in Assam Assamese is used as Language of communication. However a bit of broken Hindi is also used in practice. People are fond of Dance and Music. People here have been seen playing the instrument which they had made on their own. According to the census in 2001, only 64 percent of people are literate in Assam. Out of that 72 percent are men and 56 percent are women. Post Independence saw several school, colleges and universities opening in Assam. These are engaged in educating the people of Assam. Due to the spread of education, a wave of enlightenment has run through the Assamese society. Like the other Northeastern states, the Assamese society too takes interest in various sports activities. Several sportsmen have even proved their excellence in the International Sports.

Most of the festivals of rest of the India are celebrated

here. But *'Bihu'* is the main festival. Bihu is celebrated thrice in a year- (1) *Rangali Bihu (Bohag Bihu)* (2) *Bhogali Bihu (Magh Bihu)* (3) *Kangali Bihu (Kati Bihu)* Bihu's are all agriculture-based festivals. *Rangali Bihu* is celebrated to greet the Assamese New Year that is in April. Bihu in various forms can also be seen celebrated among other tribes. Bodo community worship *'Kherai'* besides, in the months of June–July, the *Ambuvachi Mela* of Kamakhya Temple a special attraction. Moreover the *'Mela* of *Shivaratri'* in the Umanand Temple situated in the middle of Brahmaputra in Guwahati is also the main attraction. However, the change in modern lifestyle has made a dent in these communities also. The use of liquor has become a usual affair amongst the youth. There was once a time when tribes and non-tribes dwelt together but now, gradually, distrust and terrorist activities have constructed a barricade between them.

Normally, Assam has a patriarchal society however women have their appropriate place. During various festivals females dance and sing along with their male counterparts. Child marriages are almost negligible here. However, the communities do marry amongst themselves but generally it does not happen always. The custom of elopement before marriage is also prevalent. Before Assamese societies preferred to stay in joint families but with the spread of education and industrialization, the concept of single families has germinated. In Assamese community, one can divorce with mutual consent but Institute of marriage is so strong that such cases are rarely seen.

Economical Constitution

The economy of the biggest Northeastern state -Assam is based on agriculture and around 75 percent of the population is directly or indirectly associated with it. Most of the agricultural activities are for the livelihood. Especially the farming of *'Jhoom'* in the hill area is one of the examples. Besides, the farming of Paddy, fruits and flowers are also done. Jute (Patsan) and sugarcane crops are also grown. Moreover forest resources also help in the improvement of the economical conditions of Assam.

As far as the mineral resources are concerned, although Assam is rich in Petroleum, Natural Gas, Coal and Limestone; yet it's not developed industrially. State has three refineries. And in 1999, fourth refinery was established. Besides, with the intention of boosting industrial growth in Assam, Central Government has endeavoured to start fertilizer factories, cement factories and several electricity units. According to the data in 1980-81 the average income of an individual in Assam is Rs. 6663. The contribution of Agriculture in the development of Assam is 39 percent when around 63 percent of people are involved in agriculture and its related activities. Therefore the overall economic development of this state is compulsory. For the development of agriculture, Assam Rural Infrastructure and Agricultural Services Project (A.R.I.A.S.P), with the help of World Bank is working since September 1995. Under this plan out of total Rs. 567.65 crore Rs. 126.6 crore have been granted for agriculture.

Natural Resources

In the country Assam is the only state, which has maintained its natural greenery with its own efforts. These forest help not only in flaunting its Natural grace but also contribute towards strengthening the economic condition of the state. Several varieties of valuable timbers are found in the forest. According to a survey state has total 44 Plywood factories, around 400 sawmills, one matchbox factory and several Bamboo industries. But after Supreme Court banned on the cutting of the trees in the North East most of these factories are defunct since December 1996.

According to the 1997 survey, around 30,000 Sq. Km of area comes under forest region. In the districts of the plain areas the responsibility of forest management lies on the state forest department. Where as, various independent councils hold the responsibility of forests of hill region. State has abundance of valuable Timber apart from Bamboo and firewood. The ban on the cutting of trees is although being looked after by the forest department, however the forest mafias are illegally, cutting and selling of the trees, which is resulting into environmental hazard. Plantation of 150 Lakhs of Plants/per year have been targeted to increase the number of trees, which help in the spread of forests.

A part of Assam's forests comprise of wild animals. Single horned Rhinoceros are found here. Besides White feathered birds, Golden apes and chimpanzees are also found. To save these animals state government has constructed five nationals parks- Kaziranga, Manaas, Nameri, Dibru Saikhova and Orang. Moreover 21 Zoos are also established. In the Manaas National Park, to save Indian tiger, work is going on, within the tiger project.

Electricity System

Assam has a great capacity of producing electricity within which Hydroelectricity and even Thermal electricity can be produced. Under the thermal comes the coal or gas based units. Having such great capacity of electricity production, the state has a very low rate of its development and that's why according to 1998-99 data only 514 MW electricity was available as against the requirement of 531 MW of electricity.

An electricity unit of the capacity of 572.49 MW has been established in Assam. But it is unable to cater to the requirement of the whole state. According to 1995-96 surveys, per person consumption of electricity here is 100 K.W.H. Even the village electrification programme is moving at a very slow pace.

The state has the production capacity of 572.40 MW but not more than 200 MW/day of electricity is being produced. There are several reasons attached to it. The total capacity of the Thermal power unit at Namroop is 133.5 MW, which requires modernization. Similarly, the capacity of Bogaigaon thermal power unit has the capacity of producing 240 MW, but condition of this too is somewhat similar. The plan of the development of Namroop electrical unit is in the pipeline, besides some other electrical units are also underway. NIPCO has established an electrical plant in Kathalguri, which is even operational now. On similar lines, in the direction of starting the Amguri thermal power project (240), the plans are being worked upon.

State also has tremendous probability of hydro electricity. Keeping in view these probabilities, state government has consented towards the start of Karbi Langpi Hydal Project. However, several obstacles have come on the way of its commencement. Besides the state government is paying its attention towards the improvement of the electricity condition in state by implementing on several interstate projects. The electricity centers under Assam State Electricity Board (ASEB), have been taken for rehabilitation and modernization. The Government is seriously thinking upon inviting the private companies in the electricity area. Considering the scarcity of electricity in the state, it is taking it from Meghalaya. Due to the lack of adequate power system, industrialists are not very keen on establishing industries here. Therefore it is required for government to pay more attention in this direction.

Mineral Resources

Assam enjoys a distinctive position with regards of its mineral resources. Apart from Petroleum and Natural Gas, Coal and Limestone are found in abundance. According to 1998-99 surveys, the total production of Petroleum was 52 Lakh 71,000 metric tones. The first oil well was found in Digboi during 1889-90. In 1899 Assam Oil Company was formed. Right now total 4 refineries are operational in Assam. They are Digboi, Noonmati (Guwahati), Bogaigaon and Numaligarh. Numaligarh Refinery was established in 1999.

Because of Petroleum Industry, Fertilizer industry was

established in Namrup. Besides the state has abundant store of Limestone. In 1998, 1254 million cubic meter of Natural Gas was extracted in Assam. Same year 6 Lakh 62,000 metric tones coal was also produced.

Agriculture and Gardening

89 percent of total population of Assam lives in villages and from amongst these 65 percent of people are indulged in Agriculture or related activities. We observe that the 39 percent of economical structure is satisfied from the agricultural area. The main crop of Assam is Paddy. According to 1995-96 surveys there was the total production of 33.90 Lakh tonnes of paddy. Wheat is also being grown in the state. In the area of cash crops, the production of Jute is also very important. During 1996-96, 8.03 knots were produced. Same way the farming of potato, sugarcane, Maize and others are also done quite well. Currently, farming of several crops are being carried upon in around 39.26 Lakh hectares of land area, Paddy alone occupies 65 percent share, besides cereals and oilseeds are also grown. State has especially implemented several plans for the development of paddy.

Apart from oil production, the other thing Assam is known for is Tea. It has the maximum number of tea gardens (860). The tea farming occupies 2 lakh 2800 hectares of land area. During 1997, around 42 Lakh 54,000 tones of tea was produced. Thus tea plays an important role in the development of the state.

Silk Culture/ Breeding

In the state, production of silk and the culture of its worms are done mostly in the village regions. Traditional people cultivated the silk worms on the mulberry trees. They get silk threads from the cocoons. From these silk threads, Pat, Iree and Munga, varieties of silk is produced. There was a time once when each women of a household used to be a weaver and would weave the clothes for her family. A survey says that 30 percent of the population are associated with silk industry. Leaving two hill regions, the entire district of Brahmaputra valley has silk industry or related industries. In the Manchester of Assam Sualkuchi, there is a biggest market of silk clothes. State Government along with Central Silk Board is indulged in its development. Khadi and Village Industries play prominent role in strengthening the state economically. People not only weave clothes to suite their needs but also sell them in the local markets. Many khadi production centers are operational. Mainly among those are Belsar (Nalbari) Adabari (Kamrup) Baropujia (Nagaon). Khadi Board is also providing training for pottery and Bamboo products; thousands of villages have been employed here.

Industries

Assam lags behind in the field of industries. It's a

Oil refining plant

strange fact that a state rich in the production of petroleum and tea, lacks in the related industries. The four refineries of the state Noonmati, Digboi, Bogaigaon and Numaligarh are that of raw oils. Oil India Ltd and ONGC work towards the exploration of oil wells whereas the Assam Gas Company, Public Sector Unit of Gas Authority of India Ltd works towards the supply of Natural gas to various industries.

The state has total three big paper factories. Among which two belong to the public sector, Hindustan Paper Corporation. Two small units of fertilizers have been established near Guwahati. There are 44 plywood factories in Assam, which contributes towards the 60 percent of total country's production. State government has declared a new industrial policy in April 1997. Under this policy the government has laid stress upon the availability of infrastructure facilities to establish industries. Following its implementation, two industrial development centers were started at Balipara (Shonitpur district) and Matia (Gwalpara district), where as export development Industrial center were established in North Guwahati. Besides software Technology Park was established in Guwahati. The work of Assam Gas cracker project is also in its last stage. For the development of industries,

Oil Refinery Unit

Assam Industrial Development Corporation (AIDC) was established in 1965 and it has till date helped more than 60 projects.

Road and Transportation

Post Independence saw an improvement in the field of Road and transport. It was difficult to reach Assam, as it remained cut off from rest of the country for many years. Under ground transport system have been developed in the state. Three long bridges were constructed on Brahmaputra. At first, the Saraighat Bridge joining

Guwahati and North Guwahati was constructed in 1963. Similarly the bridge joining Kaliyabar and Bhomoraguri was inaugurated in 1987. The third bridge Narnaryan Setu was inaugurated in 1998. This bridge joins Panchratna in South and Jogighopa in North. Among these Saraighat and Narnarayan Setu are Rail cum road bridges whereas bridge of Kaliabar and Bhomoraguri are the road bridges.

In Assam, Borjahar (Guwahati) Rorira (Jorhat) Mohanbari (Dibrugarh) Lilabari (North Lakhimpur) Salonibari (Tezpur) and Kumbhigram (Silchar) have airports. Due to the problem of road transport Central government has subsidized the air fares for the North Eastern states. Besides Private companies are supposed to provide 25 percent of their flights to the North Eastern states.

The condition of road transportation in Assam is quite satisfying. The state has total 32,151 Km long PWD roads, in which 2,033 Km long road comes under National Highway. Assam has roads connecting it with rest of the North Eastern states. The buses of Assam state Transport Corporation are available for transportation. Besides the state government has also arranged for Ferries (Ships). For the transportation of goods, ships are there between Guwahati and Calcutta. Many areas still lack the facility of transportation. The government is required to pay timely attention towards this problem.

Tourism

Tourism enjoys a prominent position in the state. Thousands of people from all over India visit Kamakhya temple. According to 1998-99 surveys total 1 Lakh 78 thousand Indian and 3,390 foreign tourists came to Assam. Navgrah temple situated in Guwahati too attracts the devotees. The ruin of Madan Kamdev temple (constructed in 5th century) also attracts the tourists. Shiv Sagar is another point of tourists' attraction.

In any case, the wild species of Assam are the greatest source of attraction for the tourists coming here. For instance the Single horned Rhinoceros are found in Kaziranga National Park. Various birds and animals are also found here. Similarly Royal Bengal tiger, wild elephants, golden apes are found in Manaas National Park. Perceiving the importance of tourism government has already assigned it the status of an industry. To attract the foreign tourist conserved area permit has been withdrawn. That is why the number of tourists has increased in the last 5 years. Besides Hotel Industry has also profited. The tourist Bus network is among the best network in the country. All other tourist places are connected with Guwahati. To attract the foreign and Indian tourist, government is planning to organize tourists carnivals under which 'tea tourism festival' is being organized. With the help of which European communities are intended to be attracted because their communities have a special emotional relations with the tea gardens of Assam. Government is also encouraging water sports in the Brahmaputra River.

[5]
Vashnav Sect in Assam and Shrimant Shankardev

PROPAGATION of Vaishnav sect in Assam was on similar lines as the rest of India. Evidences from ancient history confirm that during the period when Gupta dynasty ruled over Madhya Pradesh, the sceptre of Kamrup was in the hands of Pushya-Burman. It appears that Pushya Burman was quite impressed with the Gupta Empire. This is apparent from the fact that he had named his son Samudra Burman and daughter Dutta after Emperor by Samudra Gupt and the empress Dutta Devi of the Gupta dynasty. Bhuti-Burman was a descendent of the same dynasty and his stone inscription exists in 'Varganga' even today. In the inscription Bhakti Burman had calls himself 'Param Bhagwat'.

An idol of Goddess Hargauri

Its script is also quite similar to the one practiced by the Guptas. The copper plates inscription of Harjar Burman of same dynasty also has the mention of Gupta era. With all the evidences and records, one could assume that. Assam had been under the influence of Gupta culture since fourth century A.D. The twelve to thirteen hundred year old ruins of Vishnu idols found in the region further confirm this assumption. The idol of Shukleshwar discovered at Guwahati and Haigreev Madhav idol of Hajo and the statues of Vishnu from Gosai Guri's are quite ancient. The stone inscription of Bhuti Burman that was found from Barganga has the idols of Shiva and Shakti along with Vasudev's carved on it. In fact, during Gupta Empire both Shaiv and Vaishnav sects existed on equal grounds and received equal support.

The Statue of Goddess Gupta dynasty was the great follower Har Gauri of Mahakal consecrated in Ujjaini. Same issue is there in Assam as well. After Guptas, Harshavardhan came to rule over Madhya Pradesh, who was a friend of Kamrup King Bhaskar Burman it is clear from the written evidence of Huan- Tsang mentioned that this king was a 'God' worshipper but had regard for Buddhist works. Here god means- *'Shiv Mahadev'.* The period of Bhaskar Burman is assumed to be 200 years after Pushya Burman. During these 200 years several kingdoms changed over. However, in Assam only one dynasty predominated through out. This dynasty claimed itself to be the descendents of Narkasur, who is said to have originated from Vishnu (in the form of *Varah*) and *Prithus.* The rulers of this dynasty were though Shiv devotees but still worshipped Vishnu. Bhaskar Burman had equal regards for all the religion. One copper plate issued by him (found by the archaeologists) has a eulogy, which has the mention of first two shlokas about shiva vandana, and the third shloka is about Buddha and the fourth shloka is devoted to *Varah Vishnu. Dhatro succhiksshititi psormbunidhe kapat kolrupasya chakramrit* shloka has eulogy on *Chakrapani Vishnu.*

After this the administration of Assam changed and went in the hands of Harjar Burman, the second descendent of 9th century. Bal Burman of 10th century was the ruler of Assam. Although he gave pre-eminence to Shiv-puja, However Vishnu (Varah form) prayers were offered with equal regards. In the 12th century, in the eulogy of Indrapal and Ratnapal this sequence was changed. First prayer was for Lord Vishnu. These eulogies had the Vishnu's vehicle Garuda, padam, shankha, and chakra engraved on them. During 12th century King Dharmpal was a renowned ruler of Kamrup who was famous for his charities. Shri Dimbeshwar has further said-probably he was the only king who was absolute Vaishnav follower. In his first inscription plate Ardhanarishwar Shiva and Varah Vishnu have been equally praised. In his second eulogy plate there is no evidence of Shiva's prayer. When he calls himself the descendent of *Varah Purush Garun Dhwaj* and bequeaths land, then giving the reference of Burman incarnation he says-

Sakal vipr bahul pradipah,
Shrimant Babhuv Madusudan Namdheyah.
Yo Balyatah Prabhriti Madhav pad padmah,
Puja prapanch rachana suchiranchkarah.

Before this Shaiv Kings were in majority even then considering themselves This was indubitable fact that although considering themselves the descendents of Narkasur they gave adequate respect to Vishnu worship.

In the aforesaid period in Assam, the *Shaiv* sect predominated in total. During those times, all the information about –'how, what, when' of the Vaishnav mode of prayers and about, philosophy of life of Vaishnav sect, all are either imaginary or based on fables. No historical evidences of the same are available. No relevant reference or inscriptions are available, except for the two Shakt, texts. These Shakt texts are - *Kalika Purana* and *Yogini tantra*. In these Shakt texts, the dignity of Vaishnav modes of meditation is secured and it is illustrated as well, or they prove themselves- exceptional. It is hard to say so or decide. In fact it is very difficult to come to any conclusion over the authenticity of these textbooks.

Kalika Puran is the creation of 10th century. According

A page of Kalika Puran

to it amongst the three powers of the '*Devi*' the second power is Vishnu. This has the mention of some of the Vasudev *Peetha* (bench) along with the rituals of *Vishnu pooja.* Perhaps, meditation centers were there in the '*Gyanmargi*' method, where as temples in the 'Shraddhamargi' method Possibly, in *Gyanmargi* system both temple and meditation cycle had been instituted. Several *vasudev Peetha* are mentioned in Kalika Puran, which were there in the Kamrup state- *Haigreev Vishnu, Manikoot* mountains (present Hajo) *Matsya Vishnu, Madhav Vishnu* on the *Rathkula* Mountain, *Mahavarah* Vishnu on *Chitra Vah* Mountain; *Vasudev Vishnu- Dikkar Vasini* valley. The most esteemed and well known amongst these are *Vasudev* and *Haigreev.*

Haigreev Vishnu is mentioned in *Bhagwat, Mahabharat*

Yogini Tantra

and *Devi Bhagwat.* In the disguise of *Haigreev*, Vishnu killed Madhu Kaitabh. Vishnu also killed a devil named Haigreev in the disguise of a fish. Haigreev had stolen and taken the Vedas to '*Patal Lok*' (Shri Mad Bhagvad). Regardless of whether these are facts or fiction, this is certain the Vishnu had incarnated as Haigreev. His temple is still there in present-day Hajo (Adriyan- Manikoot Mountain) just adjacent to this *Haigreev* temple is *Matsya Vishnu* temple.

Idol of Vishnu

In the *kalika purana* Vasudev alter's reference give the impression of Vishnu's Vamachari (leftist) form, same like 'Shakts'. Possibly like the *Bhairvi* devotees Vasudev too had meditation cycles, which have almost vanished now. The reason being Vishnav too have (*Sahastra-naam*) hundred names, *Beej Mantra*, Samput Sadhna, *Yantras* (instruments) and stamps marks. Vaishnav sects too have the reference of *Siddhis*. Therefore it seem that during the ancient period *Gyan margi* meditation was also in existence. When 'Guhya' form of meditation of 'Agam Marga' is recognized in the branch of Shaiv shakt, then the existence of covert meditation in Vasudeva can not be denied. It is possible that in this meditation system, instead of Vishnu's, ritual of Hanumana meditation must have been in use. Vasudev altars might have been established not only in Kamrup but also in the entire India. It is possible that the colour of mystery intensified mostly in Kamrup. This is also possible that *vyuhrachana* could have been given the mysterious term. The analysis of *vyuhas* - *Parmatma* (Vasudev) Sankarshan (species) Pradhyumn (mind) and Anirudh (Arrogance/self conscious) has somewhat such form, that is, more towards *Gyanmarga.* The statement of Fakryuhar on the contexts of 'Panch Ratra) Dharma's Vyuha pooja is mentionable-

Importance of *Sanhitas (Panch Ratra)* is of two kinds within these samhitas the entry of shakt principles under Vaishnav religion- is the first description. And the second is that the Sanhitas present a sequential collection of Vaishnav beliefs and rituals. Their code of conduct is an advanced version of epic 'Mahabharata's- *Narayaniyo Pakhyanam's* school of thought in which shakt elements are intact. The 'Yantra and Mantra' are the integral part of Shakt religion. Even 'Panch Ratra' (Samhitas) too have the collection of several performances- Hypnotism, *Mantra, Yantra* etc. Even the study of Beej mantras have been done in Sanhitas quite carefully.

It appears that the whole nation was enclosed in the Shakt colour of *Panch ratra Vaishnav* religion.

We have already mentioned about the Vaishnav culture in Kamrup in 12th century. But the most indubitable evidence of 19th century is Madhav Kandali authored 'Ramayana'. All the stone inscription and evidence seems nothing as against it. This is the first 'Ramayana' written in Assamese language that is presented by Madhav Kandali on the basis of the basis of the story of Balmiki's Ramayana'. Kamban and Tulsi came after him.

The development of Neo-Vaishnav culture commenced from the time of Ramanujacharya. It is difficult to get the coordinated history of the vaishnav religion before this age. After 11th century AD, many communities- *Shri* community (founded by Vishishthadvait Ramanujacharya), Brahma community (Anand teerth Madhu), Rudra community, Sanat community (Dvaitacharait-Nimbark), Gaud-Vaishnav cult (Chaitanya- Achintya Bheda- Bhed) and other such movements were instigating the religious feelings of the country. By 15th century the victory mission of Vaishnav religion had completed. The last messengers of this cult were - Chaitainya, Vallabh and Shankardev. The position Chaitanya Mahaprabhu enjoys in Bengal, Shankardev enjoys exactly the same place in Assam. The prominent religion in Assam in local dialect is known as- '*Mahapurushia*' but in the *shastri* language it is known as '*Ek Sharan Dharma*'.

By 15th century, Assamese had got jaded of shakt worship. The popularity of Madhav Kandali authored 'Ramayana' is the proof of this. If Kandli had intended merely to script poetry, then he would have selected the storyline of Raghuvansh instead of Valimiki's Ramayana. Ramayana must have fascinated him because he must have already accepted in his mind that Ramayana is the only illusive character with power that can take the minds and general public on the roads of up gradation.

Shrimant Shankardev is known to have headed Neo Vaishnav religions in Kamrup. He made the 'Shakti Marg' the mode of mission. There was no place for mystery meditation in Bhakti Marga; Shrimant Shankardev came to be known as Chaitanya of Bengal. He not only had sharp intellect and meditation skills like Chaitanya but also the capacity of literary creation. He was rich with multifaceted talents. His management of skills has found its expression quite intensely in poetry, Song poetry, Drama, acting, painting and other areas. In literary standing, he was the 'Tulsidas' of Assam. That is why he had been adorned with the title '*Mahapurush*'

Shankardev : Life Portrayal

Shankardev (1449-1569) was a contemporary of Chaitanya (1465-1535) and Vallabhacharya. He was born in the middle of 15th century in a very prosperous Samanta family. Born in the Kayastha community, his ancestors were the natives of Kannauj in U.P till 13th century. During 14th century his ancestors became Samantas under the Kamta rulers in the Kamta Empire. In those days Kayasthas were known as '*Bhuyan*'. The responsibility of establishing power in the slat and security of border areas from the attackers was on the '*Bhuyan*'. Some Bhunjas were from other communities too but mostly they were '*Kaayasthas*'. Their ancestors were the chiefs of the Bhuyan- *Shiromani Bhunia.*

Shankardev also had to be on this post. Taking advantage of the prevalent situation, he could have united all the Bhunjas and taken over the throne. But instead, he left the royal post and decided to follow the path of religion. After accepting this path for the social and cultural upliftment and unity, he practiced the philosophy, literature, music, acting and other such art and acquired expertise in the above areas. The artistic interests served as a bridge between the Indian public mind and Assamese public mentality. Along with poetry, grammar based Sanskrit literature; Shri Shankardev also did intensive study of Hath Yoga a branch of yoga. Long after following the path of yoga, after he had studied *Bhagvat Puran,* he quit this path and followed Bhakti path. After his wife's death, he married off his daughter and resigned from the post of *Shiromani Bhuyan* and went on pilgrimage along with some inquisitive friends. He remained on his pilgrim tour for twelve years and visited all the important pilgrimage of India. After his return after establishing compatibility between the culture and religious following in various countries, he started working on establishing compatibility between Assam's culture and civilization. That is why, he went far from his birthplace- mid Assam, towards the east and west respectively propagating the messages of his sect and finally he gave up life in Koch Bihar of North Bengal.

Talented Shankardev

Shankardev was since child hood brilliant and energetic. The meditation of Hath Yoga had made his body more powerful. Prosperous with intelligence and physical capacity, Shankardev was impressed by Shri Mad Bhagvad Puran. Before him Gorakhnath, was yet another saint, who was very popular among all the groups of society. In Kamrup, the contemporary Shaiv and Shakt culture were till then not based on the Indian philosophical principles instead were based upon fables, public faith and public meetings. The public faith based on philosophical principals always generates blind faith and cynical atmosphere. Under these circumstance, in order to bring change in the way of thinking of the people of the Kamrup state, Shankardev

Shrimant Shankardev

tried to install new principles in the minds of the people through the medium of Bhagvad dharma, on the basis of Vedanta and Sankhya philosophy. To realize his objective he gave lectures on Brahmsutra Gita Upanishad, in the same lines of Ramanujacharya and other saints. But he did not find it necessary to write the analysis.

After his return from the pilgrimage Shankardev started giving sermons on Vaishnav religion. He established the first Vaishnav math known as *'Satra'* in Bardowa. At that time the Ahom ruler was the follower of Shakt sect. On the insinuations of the religious courtesans, the royal court was infuriated with him. After that, he established the Math in Barpeta and he started spreading Vaishnav sect. Barpeta was under Kamta Empire therefore he received a lot of royal patronage. With the help of Madhav Dev, Anant Kandli and other talented disciples he completed his victory mission by spreading Viashnav religion in Assam. He wrote several Kirtans, *'Bhagvat Bhakti Ratnakar'*, *Bhakti Pradeep*, several *Bar* Geets and one act plays. He gave magnitude and a vast reach to Vaishnav literature.

Who was his teacher? It is debatable whether he had any teacher or he attained the knowledge by the study of *Bhagvat* and related texts. Nothing is evidential but this is a fact that during pilgrimage he had been associated with many Vaishnav saints men of great virtues. Most probably he did not have any preceptor.

The impact of the analysis of Sridhar Swami's, 'Bhagvat Bhavarth Deepika', in the principles of Shankardev is clearly visible. But the knowledge is self-acquired. Among his disciples Madhavdev was the best- personality wise. He was selected as his descendent. He was also a Kayastha. Shankar dev's other disciple was Damodhar Dev, who was a Brahmin by cast. After the death of the guru, Damodhar Dev did not appreciate Madhav Dev's self-directed behaviour.

Gradually he separated and formed 'Damodara community'. In this community the dignity of shaastras had been accepted. But Madhav Dev's progressive eagerness led to the neglect of Brahmin esteem and *shastriya* dignity at several places.

The source of this New Vaishnav cult was Bhagvat Mahapuran. Instead of *Vasudev Vyuti* worship of his incarnation *Rama* or *Vishnu- Lakshmi* had begun in Gupta period. However, in the era of this neo cult it became the national religion. In Kamrup Shankardev spread the worship of Krishna. He wrote songs on Rama. He wrote the play *Ram Vijay Natak*. But accepted Shri Krishna as worthy of reverence.

This neo meditation system was termed as –'*Ek Sharan Dharma*'. *Ek Sharan* means only under Shri Krishna's refuge. *Tantrik* worship and virgin worship had corrupted whole of Assam, during this period. Especially the virgin's night worship and *Ekant Sah-Jagran* (be awake throughout night; alone with the virgin) became synonyms of corruption. Therefore, In his sect Shri Krishna's worship was stressed upon. However, There was no room for Radhika (Prakritiswarupa) in this cult. Shankardev was not ready to accept- the woman element in any form in his reverence system. The name of *Bhairavi chakra* would have been changed into *Radhachakra*. For the evaluation of social morality they established a male dominated religion and lectured accordingly. According to his principle- on worldly level, Shri Krishna is a child God of Braj. He is a friend of Arjun, and is an abductor and husband of Rukmini. His pen doesn't even spare the honest Shri Krishna. However on the philosophical level, Shri Krishna is not an incarnation but He is a *Param Brahma*. This is also the view of *Bhagvad puran*. Generally all Vaishnavist accept Dvaita to some extent but are the followers of Advaitism. Shankardev supports Bhedha- Bhed like Dvait in Advait,- 'God is Dvait in a sence but Advait in another. At that particular moment He attains a particular disposition.

There is no regard for the sixteen step method of the worship system. Here '*Hari Vigrah*' or God's idol is not required, neither a *Shaligram*-like in other Vaishnav religions. The followers of the religion worship 'Bhagvat Puran' like Sikhs's worship '*Guru Granth* Sahib'. It is fair enough if there is a god's statue otherwise too an idol is not required. Thus, Shankardev sect is not against idol worship. In Kirtans, he praises Ram and Krishna in the kirtans, where as during his meditation he imagines the idol of *Narayana*. The portrayal of god's Dhyan in 'Dhyan Varnan' is given as :

Baikuntha name aache mahathan
sari-sari ranje vimananchay
vaidury hira markatmay
chandr sury jan prakashe ati
na jani yaay paase din raati
chaaru sarovar nirmal jal
sugandh padma sobhe utpala
aache rajhans samuhe ranji
lilae mrinaal bhunje ubhanji
paave paarijaat malay baab
chatak tyaje sulalit raav
bhramar gane gaave harigeet
vaishnav jane suni aan vit.

Shankardev has considered *Kirtan* (devotional songs) better than meditation. He gives utmost preference to the *Nam* Kirtan. *Nam Dharma* is yet another name for '*Ek Sharan Dharma*'. The *Bij mantra* of this community is also *Nam mantra- 'Ram Krish Hari Narayan'*. Shankardev wrote a religions book named '*Kirtan*'. It is the collection of *Pauranic* Shri Krishna and Rama related stories. This book is in the form of '*Gun Sankirtan*'. The book holds even greater value than *Bhagvad Puran. After* this the other creation of Shankardev is '*Nam Ghosha*'. Some Guna Sankritan and some *Nama sankirtan can* be found in this creation. Interestingly, in each Ghosha, the first and the last part of it, is just the repeat of names. Middle part is translation of quality (*Gunanuvad).*

After *Nam* songs, singings of *Bar* Songs have immensely contributed towards increase in the popularity of

Shankardev. *Bar* Songs are clearly inspired by the Vaishnav poetic style. These *Bar* songs are generally songs of humble self-requests :

panve pari hari karho kaatari, pran rakhbi mor
vishaye vishdhar vishe jarajar jeevan naa rahe thor
athir dhan gyan jeevan yauvan
athir yahu sansaar
putra parivaar sabahi asaar
karbo kaahe saar
kamal dal jal chitta chanchal
thir na rahe til ek
naahi bhayo bhav-mange
hai-hari
param pad par tek
kahat shankar e dehu shripati
paar kara hrikesh
tuhu gati mati dehu shripati
tatva path updesh

The language of above extract is Braj buli, its not pure Assamese. If one tries to read it like Devnagiri script the flow gets interrupted. But Assamese script has a continual flow while speaking. See second example :

paamar man raam charan chit dehu
athir jeevan raam madhav kerinam
maran sambal lehu

Krishna kinkar bhan raam param
prabhu maranahi sang na chora
avnish sevahu raam param prabhu
rahu chhavi pankaj bhora.

In Shankardev community 'Shravans' stand after the Kirtan. After listening to Shrimad Bhagvad all the evil deeds are sanctified- this is the general belief. The orthodox *Mahapurushia* family do not perform the *Shradh* of the dead person instead listen to the story of *Bhagvad.* Krishna and Shravan both elements are related with Bhagvad. In the Kirtan group women are not suppose to sit with men.

Shankardev never consecrated any woman in his entire life. On the social level the people of this community organized 'Emotional plays' after *Kirtans*. *Bhavaria* or 'Bhavna' or Ankiyanat are the -one act plays based on the short *Pauranic* stories chorus (*Sahgan)* occur on intervals. Created in Brajbuli poetry and Assamese- Brajbuli mixed prose, these one act plays still predominate the human psyche in Assam. Shankardev wrote several ' *Ankya Nat'* but only three achieved the literary standards of literature -'*Ram Vijay' Rukmini-Haran* and *Parijat-Haran*. Their style matches to that of '*Ras'* of Bihar and UP '*Yatra*' of Bengal and '*Yakshagan*' of Andhra Pradesh.

[6]
Language and Literature of Assam

THE modern Indian languages have originated from Prakrit or from the dialects of the language. The Indian Aryan languages are Hindi, Urdu Bangla, Marathi, Gujarati, Udia, Assamese, Rajasthani (a branch of Hindi), Punjabi, Sindhi, Pashto, and Kashmiri and the Dravid languages are Tamil, Telgu, Kannad and Malayalam. Pt Jawaharlal Nehru has also acknowledged the fact in his 'Discovery of India'.

The heritable rule of Assam has an apparently impinged on the states language and literature. People from the outside of the border of Assam and their culture came and assimilated here and with time it developed into a new language called Assamese. Assamese means language of Assam and people speaking this language.

The origin of the prevalent language of Assam is difficult to determine but it can be concluded that Assam's heritable empires have clearly impinged on it. Coming from Assam's border states, the aggressors- Bodos, Hill people of Mongol community, Austrics, associated with Khasi community, along with neophyte Ahoms, a remarkable sub caste of Shan tribes, all these together created a new Assamese language during the beginning of this century or during the first decade of the century. People coming from Bihar and north Bengal brought along Magadhi, Prakrit and slang, and the Arya Assamese language was formed. The Shans (Ahoms), who came from higher-Brahmadesh, the empire, which they formed after conquering a part of the state in 1228 AD, they had called it-'Assam'. In 1874, when British took over and created a new state, they called the whole state- "Assam". Austro Asian, Aryan Dravid and Mongol and other several castes contributed towards creation of this diverse language. But the credit mainly goes to Aryans and their influence. According to the evidences, Maithili language played a vital role to shape the language into its social form.

According to Huan-Tsang who travelled to Kamrup in 7th century- 'There is a little disparity between the language of central India and the language of ancient Kamrupa. This statement proves that 'Magadhi' language was prevalent in Kamrupa. According to Dr. Griyarson, who is a researcher of language in Assam and North Bengal- 'Assamese language was mainly 'Magadhi' dominated, which is same as ancient eastern Prakrit. To the east of Magadh, - Gaud or Prachya dialect was prevalent. The axis of which was Gaur of present Maldah district. This vernacular extended towards south and Southeastern parts and became the mother of modern Bangala language. At the same time the same Gaur dialect had spread towards North Ganga in the east. Currently, Assamese, represents this vernacular, in North Bengal and Assam'.

It is observed that, the synonyms of some of the words of the languages of Hindi, Maithili, Udia, and other western languages have been found in the Assamese language.

Some of the Assamese words are related to Marathi language. It is strange though that these words are not found in Hindi language. It appears that during ancient times these two states had some associations or this phenomenon must have came about due to the expansions of some dynasties otherwise it is difficult to establish such close language affiliation.

Dr. B. Kakaati in his 'Assamese-Its Shape and Development' has mentioned about the words found in the Assamese, which are supposed to have been borrowed from

Indo-Chinese community. They can be subdivided in this way :-

(1) Austro-Asian (Asian) :-

(a) Khasi (b) Kolari (c) Malai

(2) Tibetan Burmese :- Bodo

(3) Thai :- Ahom

All the Non Aryan elements of Assam valley and North Kachhar have assimilated within this. Ahom, Khanati, Turag, Fakiyal and Nova belong to Siamese-Chinese language community. Currently this community is found in Eastern Assam.

The Tibetan-Burmese community is the biggest of all the language communities in this state. And among these, Bodo language community is the biggest. Kachhari Koch, Rabha Hojai, Lalung, Garo and Matak and Chutias-all these people to some extent are part of this great language community. Most of these speak different dialects. But every one contributes towards the creation and development of Assamese language. The Bodo language community is located mainly in the Brahmaputra valley. Leaving the Khasi-Sileng language community, nearly all hill communities belong to Tibetan-Burmese language community.

After Ahoms entered into Assam and having conquered it they brought in use their own language. This language was one of the dialects of Shan family. And Shan family's Siamese-Chinese language, belonged to the Indo-Chinese language group. The Ahoms ruled over here for around 600 years. There are some remains Ahom words in Assamese vocabulary such as *Lang*-Back, *Pang*- Mine, *Pukha*-Branch, *Kareng*-Palace; and some words associated to rivers or places are –Nam-Roop, Nam-Saang, Nam-Daang, etc.

The imposition of Bodo community on the Assamese language was comparatively far more. Even today, the remains of the name of their places and rivers testify this fact. In the Brahmaputra valley the use of prefixes- "Di" and "Ji' before the names of the rivers Dibang, Di-Khau and Dichang, signify 'Water' in the Bodo language.

Assamese Literature

Dr. Griyarson is of the view that Assamese literature is a national yield. It has always been national and it still remains so. Like the European literature written in Greece during 800 BC, with the stories of '*Dak Mahapurush*' embarked on the antique creation of Assamese literature. This fact finds its reference in the text form. The exact age of this creation could not be known. According to - '*Assamia Sahitya Rachaane Ki*' (specimen of Assamese literature), the distinctiveness of this language leaves no doubt that this language belonged to the period before Shankardev, - Father of Assamese Literature.

It is very difficult to say anything with authenticity, about this great scholarly and popular poet. Most probably the way Greeks associated popular proverbs of their literature with 'Hajiad' and severe stories started to spread in his name, similarly here also these idioms and proverbs had been associated with this semi-antique poet. The Idioms of 'Dak' are popular not only in Assam but also in Bengal, Bihar, Orissa and Nepal. These prudent proverbs, which are mainly in prose form, instruct the general public, how and when to prepare for the activities related to agriculture, wedding or other social functions. The expression and the dictums of '*Dak- Mahapurush*' provide a view of the their period of creativity and the perceived social development. Their language also ascertains this. These expressions also throw light on the contemporary social and intellectual structure and the social and cultural traditions. Some dictums point out towards religious subjects in the form of religion principles.

Assamese literature is enriched with folk songs. Continuity and concentrated simplicity are the basic ingredients of these folk songs. Far from the touch of Brahminism, these songs are written in worldly and expressive language. These songs were sung even long before they were scripted. Their origin can be traced in the '*Bihu*' songs of the festival of nature- *Bihu*, which is celebrated in mid April.

Like the '*Alhas*, the forest songs of western woodcutters, which are somewhat like Bihu in their mood and reflection, are new forms in the field of the songs of Assamese literature. The natural surroundings, mountains, forests, rivers and plains conceived these songs impromptu. The farmer harvesting his field, the weaver farmer collecting '*Ari*' or *Munga* seeds from the shrubs of mulberry, a boats man boating with the flow of water or winding the fishing net off the soundless river, can be found singing this song pensively. These songs instigate spontaneously in the moments of selflessness or amidst liberated surge of sentiments.

'*Navaria* Songs' or songs of sailors are analogous to forest song in the manifestation of self-active elation. Perhaps, these songs were conceived while the sailor was just sailing with the flow of water and he as not even holding his rows.

Major John Bather had written in 1885 that makes it quiet clear :-

'Assam is a state associated with rivers. Assamese prefer to travel in small boats (*Dongis*) instead of road routes. The sailors find joy in boating because they are always engrossed in singing songs while boating.

The other types of folk songs are those, which describe the people living on the riverside. '*Barma'i*' song is the folk song of this category, in which the wife mourns her parting from her husband as he had gone to trade in the sea. The intensity of its dramatic separation reminds one of Ezra Pounds'-'Sailor's wife'.

Other than these poems of utility group, some extremely intellectual and light humoured poems are-'Pachla- Kirtan', 'Pagla-Parvati' Geet, Sipini-kirtan etc are also sung. *Pagla Parvati Geet* is sung along with a local musical instrument '*Takaari*.

Ancient Assamese literature is also rich in terms of

wedding songs and lullabies. Wedding songs or '*Biyanamas*' are full of direct or indirect references of scenes and wedding description mentioned in the epics, such as –*Har-Gauri, Ram-Sita, Usha-Anirudh and Rukmini-Krishna. These* songs generally give the thrill of poetic creations. These Pauramic songs are considered sacred. Also there are other wedding songs, which comprise of pure worldly emotions and they are expressive of young married feelings.

Among other poems, '*Lavania*' is significant in its form of creative distinctive style, Such ancient Lavanias as- *Phool-Konwar* and *Mani Konwar* are there in the Assamese literature. Before getting it in the scripted form, the singers of a particular group-'Baragi' would sing the song during festivals or some functions. Both these *Lavaniyas* are emotional, finest in expression, simple and adorned with all the literary embellishments. Like the French songs 'Rolan' developed in the third century, these, *Phool Konwar and Manikonwar* had been developing for centuries encompassing within them the pictures of various levels of social development.

The contemporary philosophy has been published in the poetry in the form of two sections. Both the schools of thought were ornate and spiritual, and would propagate simultaneously. '*Bar Geet*' also known as '*Vaishnav Bhakti*' song, were spiritual in the context of feelings and intentions, and intellectual in the context of its subject. His voice was different from that of the contemporary prevalent sentiment. In his-'Bar geets' Madhav Dev has described child form of Krishna. And Brajdham has been depicted as Shrikrishna's pauranic poetic, place of activity. This land of childhood, has the elders as *Gopis* and *mata Yashoda. The* image of Krishna, is shown not as a romantic youth playing the symbolic flute rather He is depicted in the form of child wearing-*paijani* (anklets).

A group of poets had the opportunity to stay in the court of Koch kings. These kings were very powerful they ruled for several years and contributed greatly towards the spread of education. One of the greatest kings of Koch Dynasty King Vishwa Singh extended his empire to far off lands and became the king of Kamtapur during 15th century. Under the patronage of these kings, a non-Vaishnav poet -Durgabar wrote several songs based on the dance songs '*Ojapalli*' and the folklores of '*Behula*'. He also wrote songs based on the stories of Ramayana. These songs came to be known as *Durgabari* songs.

Narayandev is one of the contemporaries and follower of Durgabar sect of this period. The way Durgabar's songs are known as Durgabaris, same way Narayandev songs came to be known as *Suknani*. Narayandev's-'*Padmpurana*' is an artistic epic in which Behula's plight and fickleness of her mind is described. Mankar is the second poet of the same branch, who kept himself away from the flourishing tide of Vaishnav and non-vaishnav poetry. There is difference of 'sentiment' between vaishnavist and non-vaishnavist poetry. If the poetry of first category has the predominance of spiritalism and sentiments, the other category has ornate and worldly desires and feelings. One is, in fact devout inspirational and the other is worldly and materialist. In short, *Bargeet* is spiritual in nature and *Mansa* and *Sheetal* are related to religions activities. The '*Bhanitas*' of '*Dak Mahapurush*' are practical and '*Banageet*' and '*Bihugeet*' are in fact personal creations.

Vaishnav Literature

Although a huge portion of ancient Assamese literature comes under folk songs, still the credit of scripting the Assamese literature for the first time goes to- Hem Sarswati, who according to Sir E.A. Gate was the poet of 13th century. He had the patronage of king Durlabh Narayan, the famous patron of knowledge and literature. His literary life started with '*Prahlad Charita*'. As the poet himself has told that the storyline of this book has been taken from Vaman Puran.

Harihar Vipr, Kaviratna Saraswati, Madhav Kandali and Hem Saraswati and other poet are the first, light of the glorious origin of Viashnav literature. A huge part of ancient Vaishnav era (1200-1400 AD) is placed in the contextual stories scripted on basis of ancient epics such as- *'Ashawamedh Parwa' 'Jaidrath Vadh'.*

Rudra Kandali of ancient Vaishnav era did the Assamese translation of *'Drona Parva'* of Mahabharata and under the supervision of King Mahamanikya; Madhav Kandli translated Ramayana into Assamese language. Because of his astounding music in the translation of the great epic, Madhav kandli became famous as an endowed person. Shankardev, the founder of Vaishnav era Assamese literature praised him as- 'matchless poet'. As the powers, propagating literary development and due to the sympathies of the local public the literature of Vaishnav era predominated West Assam. It's indubitable that the period of king Nar Narayan's rule was an era of awakening for Assamese life and literature.

The first Great Assamese Poets

The two great poets of Assam Shankardev (1449-1569) and Madhadev (1489-1596) were the medieval poets. Period wise, the famous Sanskrit Scholar Shankardev was the first great poet. He was the leading poet, as far as the quality is concerned. Coincidentally or fortunately the way precious stones are produced from ordinary stones same way his talent was stocked in Assam that touched nearly all the aspects of life. Like a religious soldier, he elatedly showed the mirror to the country, ragged with religions antagonism and soon as if awakened from sleep the public identified itself with a pleasant surprise. They not only perceived their outer reflection but also saw their inner soul form.

In the end of the century Shankardev was born, he started the writings of poetries, plays etc. based on Sanskrit texts, for the propagation of his religious beliefs and principles. His life after pilgrimage was the period of rise and creativity. He spent that period of his life, in great intellectual activities. Though he didn't remain stable at a place still, he proved to be a great artist. *'Kirtan Ghosha'* is Shankardev's popular creation, which comprise of stanzas full of religious feelings and intellect. Written with a view of spreading in public, this epic extracted the spiritual thought processes and pauranic poetical stories from *Shrimad Bhagwad, Brahma-Purana, Padm Purana* etc. Whoever reads Kirtan Ghosha gets the feel of- Shankardev filled with mental supremacy. Apart from literary and artistic greatness the book of poetry has such intellectual value, which is rare to find. Some of the other of his poetic epics are- *Rukmini Haran Kavya, Bhagvad Purana Ramayana* (Uttar Kand) *Bhakti Rantnakar* etc.

Shankar dev's poetry are introspective in nature. They present the devotional field in permanent form. Shankardev also had an amazing inborn capability of translation. To develop it he gave it the art form. He served the secret philosophical elements of Shastras as they were, and changed them into poetic pearls, which is a rare treasure. He had translated some part of *Dasham Bhagwat* and his *Bali Chalan* and *Ajamil Upakhyan* etc. are extracted more or less from Sanskrit storylines.

Drama, Poetry and Religion

In these subjects Shankardev is unrivalled due to his amazing intellectual activities. After these he took over towards some bigger social developmental endevours. The Vaishnav session custom prevalent today in Assam is gift of the same endowed Shankardev, Bhavna or Sangeet Nat in the art history of the country is also legacy of this skilled scholar. He created plays based on Purana stories staged them too. His plays are *Rukmini Haran, Kalia Daman, Parijat Haran, Ram Vijay, Patni Prasad* etc. Besides the art of colourful decoration of the stage was also developed by Shankardev. The soft music sprinkled in the plays like *Rukmani Haran* reminds one of *Bargeets*. These *Bargeet* can also be called as soft poetry of fact entrapped with unique sweetness and philosophy.

Priest of Poetry and Music- Madhavdev

The disciple of Shankardev and descendent Shri Madhavdev was born in 1489, in North Lakhimpur. He died in 1596 AD in Koch Bihar. He completed the half accomplished tasks of his teacher. As Plato was the disciple of Socrates, likewise Madhavdev was a disciple of Shankardev. His creations encompassed of high-end chain of poetic principles and extensive appeal. *'Namghosha'*, *'Ramayana'*, *'Aadi Kand'*, *'Nammaalika'*, *'Vaishnav Keertan'*, *'Bhakti Ratnawali'* etc. are some of his main epics. His dramas are *'Chor Dhara'*, *'Pipra Guchuva'*, *'Bhumi Letova'*, *'Bhajan Vyavhar'* and *'Arjun Bhanjan'*.

Madhavdev was unrivalled in the field of music. He had full expertise in *Pingals*. He himself was a singer and would sing his poetries and song in his melodious voice. The way bamboo and *Narkat* plants dance during storms, likewise the audience would dance to his *Bargeet* songs.

Ram Saraswati

Contemporary route guide of Assamese literature did a great deed, by translating Sanskrit Mahabharat into Assamese language. He stands tall among the rows of heavy weights of ancient Assamese literature in the field of superior characterization, depth of perception, beauty and language power. He presented a drama poetry named *'Bhim-Charita'*. This poetry is purely Assamese in terms of its wit and humour. The Mahabharat of Ram Saraswati is not a word-by-word translation, rather a true copy of it. This translation of Mahabharata, which is in its apt meaning called as- 'Encyclopedia of Indian History, Puranas and Philosophy', opened new avenues for the poets and religious leader's creative abilities.

Anant Kandli

With the translation of Pauranic subjects he enriched Vaishnav group songs with prosperous Ragas. Although his identity remained mysteriously hidden for long period.

According to Kissane Keane-'In contrast to the poison filled cups of fragranced contemporary Sanskrit scholars, like the ambrosial container', the author of Hindi Ramayana Tulsidas, Anant Kandli being a Sanskrit scholar, preferred his own mother tongue as the medium of expression instead of Sanskrit.

Anant Kandli's *'Sahastranaam Vrittant'* and *'Dasham Bhagwat'* stands tall in the high-end category of literature due to its style and nature. The way his skills have sharpened in the battle and cosmetic description and the coordination of reality and principle described in-' *Kumar Varan'* in no other of his creations, it is so. He was a native of Hajo present in Karmrup. He along with Ram Saraswati was also the last ray of the setting sun of Vaishnav poets.

The translation of Bhagwat serves a milestone in the ancient Assamese literature. It has left deep impact in the human mind and brought the principles of religion and moral science closer to life Dr. B.K. Kakati writes-

The religious principles of Shankardev involved attention of the people and his disciples wrote several books most of which are in the poetic forms. The excitement of bringing religions text to the general public's reach was so much that some period after Shankardev, his follower Bhattdeva did the Assamese translation of whole of *'Bhagawad Gita'* and *'Bhagvad Purana'* in 1593 AD.

In short religions impact and an unstable development excitement were the main symptoms of Vaishnav era. The main doctrine of this religion was the worship of God in the form of Bhakti and Vishnu or Krishna. In the words of Pd. Hariprasad Shastri 'There was a cosmetic and spiritual progress in the personality of Krishna and the devotees received the pleasure, so that they could forget their surrounding difficulties and some people even found hearty peace forever.

Numerous creations on the subjects of- Astrology, Mathematics, vetenary diseases, dance forms, and sex related subjects serve as a milestone in the Assamese literature of former-Vaishnav period. Some of these are- Poet Shankar authored- *'Shri Hasta Muktawali'* (on the art of dancing), Sukumar Vaskat authored 'Hastividyarnav (on astrology) in 1734. Surya Khati Daivagya, in 1806 AD authored *'Ashwa Nidan'* (on horses), Kaviraj Saraswati's *'Bhaswati'* (on Astrology), *'Kitabat Manjari'* (Maths in poetic form). Besides 'Biography' writing in prose and poetry form also flourished. In Assamese language-'Biography is known as- *Charitputhi*, normally these are about the life stories of religions saints, leaders, Many biographies were written about the life of Shankardev. Most famous writer was Daityari Thakur, Bhushan Dwij, Ram Rai and Anirudh. Their biographies are the dictionaries of contemporary information.

It is not that in the prose era of North Vaishnav era the poetry was neglected. Ahom king Rudra Singh's courtesan poet Kaviraj Chakravarti (1695-1714) had done the Assamese translation of *'Geet Govind'* originally written in Sanskrit and also the complete analysis of the same. The other of his on Sanskrit based creation- *'Shakutala Kavya'* is a poetical story. *'Mrigavati Charit'* by Ramdwij is a poetry based on unusual folklore, which resembles to one of the Hindi poetry of 15th century. In fact, the era after 17th century became a part of the history. The transform is significant in the sense- prose took the place of poetry.

Modern Assamese Literature

The history of modern Assamese literature is a new development. In 1816, after the British brought about some political changes and their later on with their educational reformation policies, it began. Simultaneously entered the western literary streams, styles and standard and they got settled in the new literature of British period. The Literature all the regional languages of this period received inspirational treasure from foreign countries especially from Great Britain. Mr. Latif and Mr. P.R. Sen tell how it has influenced the Urdu and Bengali literature. Yandabu Treaty politically ended the ancient customary method and western education finished it intellectually.

The Neo directors of new age of Assamese literature belong to 'American Baptist' Mission. Assamese literature saw the birth of poetry literature with the publishing of Bible in Assamese. In 1818, Atmaram Sharma of Nagaon translated the Bible and Baptist Mission of Shrirampur, Bengal, published it. This was a period of struggle for Assamese language. Bengali had replaced Assamese language from local offices and schools. During the British Empire the British offices were full of Bengali speaking people; thus Assamese was deceivingly uprooted and its lawful position in courts and educational institutes were taken away. Assamese language not only lost its rightful position but also its desire to stay and evolve.

The responsibility to rescue Assamese went on to American Baptist Mission. It gave its official position and recognized it in all its institutes. Forced by the compulsory circumstances Sir George Campbell's Government started an investigation on the demand of recognition of Assamese language by the government. In 1853, a judge of Calcutta High Court Mr. A..J. Mofut Mills was assigned to give all the information on Assam. In 1855, his paper was published.

'As an English youth who does not learn English properly, cannot be taught Latin, likewise an Assamese should not be taught any foreign language till he knows his own language'. Finally Assamese was recognized as state language.

In the ancient-Jonaki era, there was no direct western influence on Assamese literature. It had influence of English-Bengali stream that remained for quite long. The progress of Assamese language within the legal boundaries and the publication of monthly magazine 'Jonaki' by a student group studying in Calcutta for higher education gave a true impetus to Assam's literature withered by the relations created by North Ahom Treaty period. It is said that the thought of the publication of this paper, germinated during a Tea party. The way Plato Symposium took birth in the *Naish* Party organized by 'Agathon' poet; the role of the magazine -'Jonaki' (conceived in the same manner), in Assamese literature of British period was quite impressive. In fact, *Arunodaya* (1946) and *Jonaki* (1889), these two magazines are two milestones of modern Assamese literature which have brought constructive changes in the literary streams and art.

The end of 19th century period was of incomparable stimulation for Assam and its literature. This era had been of deep interest and great inspiration. That resulted in all the literary mayhem. A wave of optimism, outlines and innovation in art surged. The plays like –'*Bhramrung*' a translation of Shakespeare's- 'Comedy of errors' were new style play and these replaced the historic vaishnavist plays and spread the new style and subjects. The place of ancient poetry was gradually but certainly taken over by new stream of reflectionist (Chayavad) poetry. It had predominance of a diversity of ideas. Besides new plays, poetry, novels, stories, essays etc entered the literary stream.

Just before this renaissance period Assamese literature was more or less inclined towards preaching. Under Jonaki's supervision, it was deprived of its ancient religious and other perceptive powers. During this period, literature was for the first time made humanist.

Bholanath Das and Ramakant Chaudhary were the guides of the practice of non-rhyming poetry and they were the pioneer poets to accept the new style of non-rhyming poetry and to relegate the ancient conventional system. He provided Assamese poetry with new strength by its restoration, salvation and by expanding its boundaries.

Bholanath Das (1858-1929) published his non-rhyming poetry '*Sita Haran kavya*' in 1888 AD. 'Ramayana' is the subject matter of it. Besides the credit of the poetry collection *Kavita Mala* and *Chinta Ragini* also goes to him. These were published in 1882-83 and 1884 respectively.

In the Assamese literature they were the best among the new system of song poetry. A new and different style of poetry in the form of song-poetry system is the greatest gift of this century. Nature based song poetry *'Megh'* of Bholanath Das places the poetry on a sturdy foundation and sets a new example in the field of poetry.

Ratneshwar Mahant who wrote *'Ganwalia Bowari'* (village daughter-in-law) and Baldev Mahant, who wrote *'Kauri Aroo Siyal'* (Crow and Jackal) and Bali Narayan Bara who wrote *'Asamiya Babu'* and *Dangeria* (Mr.) are the leading poets of ironic poetry in the Assamese literature. Their ironic poetry is neither personal nor contextual nor intellectual. Rather these are social and influential as well. If the credit of making ironic poetry popular among masses goes to Bali Narayan Bara then Kamlakant Bhattacharya popularized Nationalism as the subject of Assamese poetry. In fact he was the architect of nationalism through the medium of literature.

In the collections of *'Chintanal'* and *'Chinta Tarangini'* Kamlakant Bhattacharya's poetry and his essays in *'Ashtavakra'* are equally famous for their impact and mental vitality. He had contributed greatly towards Assamese literature. He is enriched with quality and braced with ideas.

The contemporary of 'Jonaki' and 'Bijuli' era- Padmnath Gohain Barua is famous for his prose creation *'Shri Krishna'* and poetry *'Lila Kavya'* that was written after the sudden demise of his wife. *'Ganv Buddha'* is his second famous creation. Song poetry collection *'Jurni'* was published in 1900 AD, which brought him in the category of exceptional poets. During his period many plays were also written. These were as such- *'Kaniyar Kirtan'* of Hemchand Barua, *'Ram Navmi Natak'* of Gunabhiram Barua and Venudhar Rajkhova's *'Tini Ghaini'* Venudhar Rajkhova is amongst the elderly writers and is known for the creation of *'Chandra Sambhav Kavya'* many songs, song poetries, besides several prose creations.

Important people of the second group are Lakshminath

Bejbaruah, Hemchandra Goswami and Chandra Kumar Agarwala. The natural development of human mind is possible in the era, which with time frees itself from the ancient orthodox ties. The contemporary German literature of Gete is festooned with such new flowers. 'Jonaki era' also, along with its two route guides -Agarwala and Bejbaruah, is an era of similar development and freedom. Hemchandra Goswami, who had deep interest in history and ancient elements and who was the life force of the great creation-'*Assamese Sahityakar Chanaki*' was the third pillar of the tripartite of Bejbarua and Agarwala. Goswami's '*Phular Chaki*' came out as series in the magazine- '*Assam Bandhu*' which was published in its present form in 1907 AD. Besides he was also the leader of 'Sonnets' in Assamese literature.

Along with Hemchandra Goswami's '*Puva*' poetry, Nature poetry too came into existence as a section of song poetry. Later on great talented nature poet Raghunath Chaudhuri reached it to the crest of success. '*Sadri*', which comprise predominantly of naturalist song poetries is a bold expression of this poet.

Apart from this, there are other poets too who have written on nature. In the English romantic poetry tradition all these poets have imagined the nature as full of life force vivacity and activity.

Due to the western influence like the natural song poetry, aesthetic song poetry is the main bequest of this period. Their intention is to – bind desires. According to the romanticists-this is a godly feeling, which crosses the restrictions of pleasures of the senses. The aesthetic poetries of Bejbarua- '*Malti*', '*Priyatmar Saundarya*' and the folk song 'Dhanbar aur Ratni' are remarkable. '*Kadam Kali*' is the collection of his poetries.

Bejbarua is in fact a national poet who has presented some great expression of National importance. He is the author of Assamese National Music '*Ae more Aponar Desh*' like Robert Browning's- '*Pravaasi Ki Bhavana*' is a person's reverie of his homeland who is staying abroad on his own will.

The credit of the creations '*Belimar*', '*Chakradhwaj Singh*' and '*Jaimati Kunwari*' (1915) plays goes to Shri Bejbarua. These are all historical plays.

Chandrakumar Agarwala is a writer of philosophical poetries. He was a philosopher, before being a poet. Among such poetries- his two collection '*Pratima*' and 'Bin Baragi' are full of philosophical feelings.

Yatindranath Dubra, who has to his credit the creation of song poetry collection '*Apon Sur*' and the other '*Banphool*', was extremely popular amongst aesthetic poets. His perception is serious.

Being quiet young, age wise, the author of aesthetic poetry-'*Papri*' and '*Swapna Bhang*' Ganesh Gogai is a contemporary of Dev Kant Barua- poet of 'Sagar Dekhisa'. He was the last among the chayavaadi poets. The way a Japanese embellishes his blue bouquet with cherry and chrysanthemum flowers, keeping the independence of colours and their glory intact, similarly he is god gifted with the talent of expressing imagination and feelings.

The author of the poetry collection '*Shevali*'- Ratna Barkakati, comes under the category of Agarwala in terms of aesthetic pôetry and philosophical prose creation. Among the mystery poets, the poetess of '*Sandhiyar Sur*' and '*Saponar Sur*' Nalini Bala Devi and the author of 'Tumi'- Ambika Giri Roychaudhari are unrivalled. Ambika Roychaudhari is also the poet of Nationalist lyrics. His '*Karaagar Geet*' is a collection of such poetry on the other hand Nalini Bala Devi is a spiritual loner. She is a mystery poetess not because of particular religious contact rather because of her nature and insight.

Assamese Women Authors

Instead of Nalini Baladevi and Ambika Roychaudhari, the author of '*Jyoti Kana*' Neelmani Phukan is closer to the Agarwala in its mysterious and philosophic mentality. His '*Mansi*', is a valuable poetical collection. It is a kind of symbol of absolute beauty. Durgeshwar Sharma is yet another poet of mysterious and philosophic lyrics. Other popular poets of the same branch are Chandradhar Barua, Padmadhar Chaliha, Vinand Barua, Dandi Nath Kalita, Mitradev Mahant, and Mafijjudin Ahmad Hajarika Shaildhar Rajkhova. Apart from Nalini Bala Devi other famous poetesses are- Yamuneshwari Khatniyaar, Dharmeshwari Devi, Divya Bharaali, Fatima Khatun, Vimala Rajkhova and Shuchivrata Roychaudhari. Prose and novel writers are- Padmavati Phuknani, Chandraprabha Saikia, Snehlata Bhattacharya, Padma Kumari Gohain, Suprabha Goswami and Indira Goswami.

Prose and Essays

In the field of prose and essay writing Dr. Banikant Kakti enjoys renowned position. His 'Purni Assamia Sahitya' is an evidential critical study. If we use the words of Voltaire about Shelly then these prose writings are written in-' clear, vigorous and amicable' style. There seems such profundity of intellect and critical insight that is rarely found anywhere else. Dr. S.K. Bhuma's biographical study-*'Anand Ram Barua'* and Benudhar Sharma's historical study *'Maniram Dewaan'*, which is in fact written on the personality of Devan himself enjoy important place in Assamese literature. He also has to his credit writing of various essays and prose studies. Radha Phukan and Sharat Goswami are famous for their writing base on Vedanta and other philosophical writings Dr. Hem Barua who is also a Doctor by profession has created a niche in the history as a famous essayist. He writes both on light and serious both the subjects and his expertise shows everywhere the way a player keeps floating on the ice. His *'Chimpania'* and *'More Ghar Khan' are* enriched with prominent literary attraction.

One Act Plays

Among the playwright Jyoti Prasad Agarwal, who is supplemented with god gifted talents of music, poetry and art has created a Niche with his plays- *'Shonit Kunwari'* *'Lobhita'* and *'Karengar Ligiri'*. Karengar Ligiri is the best of his creations. Amongst the other playwright are the author of *'Narksur'*- Atul Hajarika, author of *'Bamini Konwar'*, Daiv Talukdar, Pravin Phukan of *'Lachit Barphukan'* Lakshya Chaudhori who wrote *'Raksha Kunwar'* and few others. In fact there are several plays and essays of the aforesaid writers those all cannot be mentioned here due to space crunch. The famous storywriter Thaka's- *'Prajapatir Bhul'* is the first one act play of Assamese literature. Between the third and fourth decade of this century it was published in the monthly magazine 'Awahan' since then such plays are being written that has tremendously contributed in the store of the Assamese drama literature.

In 1948 AD, All India Radio Centre, Shillong -Guwahati was established and simultaneously radio drama also started in the Assamese literature. There is a slight difference between Radio drama and One-act play. They are not entirely similar.

'Bhograj', *'Adha Aka Chabi'*, *'Jinti'*, *'Malti'*, *'Erabatar Sur'* and other radio dramas have extended the confines of Assamese literature. All India Radio Centre Shillong-Guwahati inspired such plays by organizing drama festival. It is organized by the radio every year.

Novel and Fiction

The last decade of 19th century saw the inception of novels in the modern Assamese literature. Hemchandra Barua pioneered this change. His novel-*'Bahire Rang Bhitare Kova Bhari'* is a kind of social developmental novel as it satires on useless covert conventions and blind beliefs. The first novel by Rajnikant Bardolai in 1895. *'Miri Jiyari'* is a multi-structured in literary style that is why it enjoys a paramount position in the Assamese literature. His novel- *'Manomati'* is a historical fiction based on Burmese attack with an ornate story, He has given it the form of antique realism, instead of ornate escapism. *'Mirijiyari'*, located within the confines of hill tribes is a melodramatic and emotional love story. His other novels are *'Rah Dai Ligiri'*, *'Niramal Bhakt'*, *'Rangili*, *'Tamreshwari Mandir'* and *'Dandra Droh'*. Bardoai, for his contributions to Assamese literature, can be compared to Sir Walter Scott of English literature.

The social novels start only after Rajnikant Bardolai pioneers Historical novels. Dandinath Kalita's novel *'Sadhua'* with of the social backdrop and atmosphere serves as a route guide in the field of novels. The stream of social realism is continually surging and its modern expressions- Bina Barua's *'Jeevanar Batat'* R.M. Goswami's *'Chak Naiya'* Md. Piyar's *'Sangram'* Navkant Barua's *'Kapili Paria Sadhu'* B.D Goswami's *'Kecha patar Kapani'* Deen Sharma's *'Sangram'* Yogesh Das' *'Dabar Aru Nai'* characterize the world wars related social streams which are engaged in damaging each other.

Fiction is not only a short novel; and though its conciseness prepares its structure still other perimeters are required. Joseph T. Shipli says-

'Completeness of effect is an external subject'. The suitability of styles, events and patience are its artistic mediums. Bejbaruah and Sharatchandra Goswami are the storywriters based on the ancient theorist. Normally their stories lack the required modern story artistry. Often they seem unclear on the perimeters of story and imagination. They could just start the story era but could not provide appropriate speed to it.

As a story writer Yogesh Das has earned a lot of popularity. He has added a physiological backdrop to the social life and related various problems. Birendrakumar Bhatacharya, known for depicting village life in his stories, is famous for his art and close observation. The contribution of Indira Goswami cannot be disregarded in the modern Assamese literature. She has also been awarded with 'Gyanpeeth Award'. Other famous fiction writers are Kul Gogai, Bhabendranath Saikia, Rohini Kakati and Chandrprasad Saikia.

An apparent difference is surfacing in art and its objective of the Assamese poetry. Reconsiderations and new expressions are finding way due to the revision on Marxist Logic and Freud's psychological material science has lead to new expressions and rethinking. The excitement of ancient stationary (achalaytan) mentality diminishing and instead the modern evaluation of art has opened new horizons for the poetry. In the Pre reflectionist poetry era, the contemporary colour, beauty has diversified from the fascination described in *'Deep Shika Ka Patang Banne Vale'*. As a substitute, a new interest is formed in life and society. Now there is no room to- 'write, create or sing', about its personal interests.

TS Elliot, Ezra Pound and Dillan Thomas and some other western poets had extensively influenced modern Assamese literature. Poetry is becoming intellectual. It is being enlivened and publicized by *'Pachuva'* (now closed) *'Ramdhenu'* kind of monthly magazines. Now, when these new powers are there, they have presented several new young poets. They accepted this medium of expression and gave new dimensions and helped in the extension of Assamese Literature. In the field of modern poetry Nabhkant Barua and Hari Barkakati have touched new horizons of popularity. Few other contemporaries are- Mahendra Bara, Homen Bargohain, Ram Goagai, Keshav Mahant, Beereshwar Barua, Mahim Bara, Prafull Bhuyan, Biren Barkatki, they have shown tremendous hopes and destiny.

This era is often ascribed as the decline age of Assamese literature. However, as a matter of fact, often the womb of decline holds the seeds of development. The time cycle intakes everything in the world. World will perish but not before springing some green tendrils of a live world.

[7]
Hindi and Hindi Journalism in Assam

PRIOR TO the year 1930, only colloquial Hindi had reached this land of occult. Some say that the language was brought in by Hindi speaking migrant labourers, who had brought along with them the contemporary Hindi and eventually it became the Assamese Hindi. A little thought makes it amply clear that the language used by labourers was Bhojpuri or its vernacular, not withstanding that, since the language was brought into use in Assam, it ought to be regarded as Assamese Hindi –a home-grown product of Assam. A form of this Hindi is in colloquial use even today. To cite some of it - '*Chai Khayega Na Kya*' or '*Sah Khayega Na Kya*', '*Jal Khayega Na Kya*' or '*Pani Khayega Na Kya*' would roughly translate as "Would you like to have some tea"

Assamese is Assam's own language. The area of Assam comprised of Kamrup district and Nagaon. As such the language was used in all the 12 district of Assam but its main literature was available in these two districts only.(There are Assamese Press in Dibrugarh, Tinsukia, Digboi, Shiv Sagar, Golaghat and Tezpur. An Assamese term, *Guahati* meaning 'Market of beetle nut' - 'Guwahati", had the printing press of Assamese and English language long before. Before that Assamese manuscripts were available in Kamrup and Nagaon. Assamese language starts from the prose- poetry of Shri Bhatt Dev. This is its special feature.

The Assam before 1930 AD was stretched till 60,000 Sq mile and was entirely *'Asam'* (non plain). The way it was naturally structured, same was the case of its languages. The languages coming from outside were Bengali, Nepalese, Telgu, Rajasthani but they were not accompanied with their literature. Even, hundreds of languages like Aao, Angami, Lotha, Katcha, Sema, Kuki, Konyak and Mainpuri etc, did not possess any literature of their own. The first literary creator of Assam- Shri Bhatt Dev gave a new life to Assamese literature by translating 'Mahabharata' and Ramayana into Assamese language.

Every corner of Assam has one or the other God temple. Even the Lack of conveyance does not play any hindrance and people in millions are reaching Kamakhya, Vashishtha Ashram, Navgrah, Umanand, Parshuram Kund and other pilgrimages. Assamese literature and religions was sidelined and British took advantage of this situation. English language flourished on its own after having entered the area of Indian culture.

In 1919 AD, when *Bapu* (emodiment of national enlightenment), inspired the nation for the spread of Hindi, the nation Assamese tagged along with Hindi Nation. That is because this programme was started on national level. Param Hans Baba Raghavdas reached Assam while on his way to spread Hindi. Due to his efforts Pt Dhyandas in Golaghat, Shri Shivsinhasan in Dibrugarh and Shri Ambika Prasad in Jorhat and Shri Ram Roop Singh in Guwahati, established Hindi schools. Due to his efforts alone, Hindi schools were established in 12 districts of Assam. Finally in the Nagaon district, with the efforts of an Assamese upcoming poet Shri Dev Kant Barua, a primary school was opened. This programme is in process since then.

Assam's first Chief Minister Shri Gopinath Bardolai had planned to open a Hindi Primary School in each of schedule cast colonies; but unfortunately he died. After that three primary schools in the name of *'Rashtriya Shiksha Sadan'* were started. These were not government aided but were totally without fees and they sustained on the donation money, and with the help of local public. They are presently under the Assam Government. The in 1955 AD, Shri Saryu Prasad, then Chief Justice of Assam High Court inaugurated the building of '*Rashtriya Shiksha Sadan*' (Basic High School) but it could not sustain for long.

For that matter, some people find the episode of spread of Hindi unsuitable but even the present Assamese Hindi readers use to be surprised to find a Hindi write up on this context. The storehouse of Hindi, publicized today is full of nourishing elements. Situation is covered with resolved problems. Therefore, now- its time to ponder over the issue of spread of Hindi instead of sitting, astonished.

When Raghav Das reached Assam he suggested calling upon a meeting under the president ship of Shri Gopinath Bardolai. In this meeting, Shri Banikant Kakati, Shri Rajnikant Chakravarti, Shri Dev Kant Barua, Shri Bhuvneshwar Barua, Shri Hem Barua, Shri Dutta Barua and Hajarika conceived a programme to visit each and every village on foot to spread Hindi language. This went on till 1939 AD. After that, under the supervision of Shri Bardolai '*Assam Rashtra Bhashsa Prachar Samiti*' was formed. In 1938, late Shri Kamadevji, along with Late Shri Jamana Prasadji executed this task. Then they formed '*Assamia Hindi Sahitya Parishad*' *after* which the sun of Hindi literature rising in Assam.

Presently, the study of Hindi has started in every city of Assam. Among these Tinsukia, Dibrugarh and Guahati's Hindi High Schools are old ones. Hindi Department has been opened in Guahawti University. Same way in Tinsukia,-a Non-Government College and in Manipur, Arunachal Pradesh, Nagaland,- Government Colleges, have been established.

Although, Assam Government and Central Government have made several efforts to spread National Language – Hindi, Assam's first Chief Minister even declared several plans for Hindi's progress and prosperity and numerous nationwide language-spreading institutes are also working, yet these institutes have not been much successful in the mission of the spread of the National Language.

The strongest mediums to communicate and spread Hindi in Assam are the natives of Assam who have gone and settled there from UP, Bihar, Delhi, MP, and Rajasthan. The way these resident labourers, rickshapullers have contributed towards the spread and communication of Hindi, no National Language spreading institutes could endeavor to the same.

Hindi Journalism

Assam is a fertile land for Hindi. There are over 5 lakhs Hindi speaking people in Assam. People from Bihar, Rajasthan and UP and other Hindi speaking are areas came and settled here. This is a reason behind good consumption of Hindi dailies, weeklies and monthly newspapers and magazines. There are also many fine Hindi scholars who are originally Assamese speaking.

In 1942, the first Hindi weekly *'Akela'* was printed in Assam, which continued to exist till seventies. This weekly was published under the editorship of Shri Vishwanath Gupt. There used to be adequate material on Assamese literature in this magazine. It also printed original Assamese poetries in Devnagiri and their translation in Hindi. According to an unconfirmed information, firstly, -*'Nav Jagrarti', a* weekly of Assam was published. Under the editorship of Shri Pannalal, the publication of *'Nav-Jagriti'* started from Dibrugarh.

At the same times in 1950, Shri Devendranath Prashant started a Hindi monthly named 'Purva Jyoti' from Guwahati. He held the editorial ship of this magazine for 15 years. After that Shri Chaganlal Jain, having same eye for both Assamese and Hindi became its editor. He made it a weekly. Till 70's 'Akela' and 'Purva Jyoti' had a good readership among the Hindi readers of Assam. Shri Jain also published the first Hindi Assamese dictionary.

In 1962, Assam's first Hindi daily Newspaper '*Dainik Lokmanya*' started. Shri Ramprasad Tripathi was its editor. But due to economical restraints it could not go on for long. According to '*Hindi Patrakarita-Vividh Ayaam*' almost at the same time, a weekly named '*Meri Kalam*' closed soon after it started. '*Aaj Ka Sansar*' edited by Shri Vishvanath Upadhyaya, '*Aj Ki Aawaj*' edited by Shri Chandra Shekar Mishra, all these newspaper published from Guahati were transitory. Shri Mishra also published a fortnightly named '*Lok Sandesh*'. '*Desh-hit*' of Shri Umashankar Mishra and '*Samvaad*' of Shri Chandra Bhushan Sharma are few of prominent newspapers. Shri Sukhdev Bhai's '*Majdoor*' was a main paper of the workers. '*Prabhat*' was also similar. '*Rajdut*' (editor Shri Kamleshwar)- published from Guahati was only magazines for children. '*Nakhshatra*' a newspaper was also published from here '*Assam Bhumi*' was published from Tinsukia under the editorship of Shri Kamleshwar Upadhyaya. From the same place, under the editor ship of Raju Khemka- '*Durga Puja Smarika*' was published. It had plenty of literary materials. Shri Khemka also edited a magazine named 'Musico' in the anniversary of the institute with same name.

In 1974, Northeastern state Marwari conference-published its monthly journal- '*Samaj Vikas*' from Tinsukia. Under the editorship of- *Assam Rashtra Bhasha Prachar Samiti*'s secretary Shri Shankar Lal Sharma from Guwahati, started a weekly '*Shankarnaad*' but it was also transitory.

The Golden Era of Journalism

In the history of Assam the later part of 80's would be considered Golden period for Hindi Journalism. This time span saw the publications of three Hindi dailies from Guwahati. They are '*Purvanchal Prahari*' 'Sentinel' and '*Uttarkaal*'.

At first in may 1989- M/S GL Publication Ltd carried out, on a massive scale- the publication of eight-paged Hindi daily '*Purvanchal Prahari*'. The publication of this newspaper is being carried out under the editor ship of the managing director of GL Publication- Shri GL Agarwal. Shri Krishnamohan Agarwal was its working editor for two years. Shri Vinodanand Thakur- as an advising editor, served the newspaper for some time. Now Shri satyanand Pathak is an executive editor of this newspaper.

Thereafter in the same year in June 1989, Publishers of Assamese Daily- '*Aajir Assam*' and English daily 'Sentinel' Omega printers and Publishers Pvt Ltd started the publication of Hindi daily 'Sentinel' under the editor ship of Assamese editor Shri R.M. Bagwati. The young journalist, Shri Mukesh Kumar as a working editor involved himself to get it a standard level. He remained at this post for 2 years. Shri Chandreshwar too remained its working editor for several years.

After that third Hindi daily 'Uttarkal' was published during October, 1989, under the editorship of Shri Govardhan Prasad Atal.

Once again, G.L Publication Groups in 1991 started Hindi weekly 'Saptsetu' under the editoship of Shri G L Agarwal. The initial editor of this 16-paged tabloid shaped newspaper was Shri Vinod Ringania.

As far as the standard of these newspapers, their initial problems and their structures are concerned, it would be mandatory to say that –in a non-hindi speaking region the publication of these newspapers on such large scale (offset printing) was in fact an adventurous dealing. It is a fact, however, that these newspapers were published, keeping in view the need of the hindi speaking people staying in Assam and northeastern states; but this a fact again that with the help of these newspapers not only several languages of northeast (Assamese, Bodo, Manipuri etc) are flourishing among the readers of hindi world. And also these have set a distinctive example of cultural unity and assimilation.

Initially, these newspapers had to face threats from several terrorist groups and it appeared once that these might have to be closed down. But due to immense patience and strong determination of the owners, and with the support of Hindi readers, this could not happen. Anyway these papers are being published with unobstackled speed.

As far as the structure and standard of these newspapers are concerned, it would be appropriate to mention that the level of the get-up, make- up and the compilation of information and the printing give the feel of the National Papers. *'Purvanchal Prahari'* has the highest circulation; even 'Sentinel' enjoys a good readership. Publication of the *Uttarkaal* now close down. The total sale of these newspapers works out around 40 to 50, 000. In case of news material and selection, - *'Purvanchal Prahri'* stands better than Sentinel. Its structure, however, is regional but it provides adequate space to national news. The news materials of these newspapers include adequate information on the literature and language cultural of Assamese and other northeastern states. Hindi Translation of various languages too finds its place in these newspapers. Journalist Ravikant 'Ravi' keeps northeast literature at the focal point and is publishing a monthly magazine named '*Ulupi*', which is commendable.

The forte of these newspapers is that they extensively use the assimilation of common vocabulary of prevalent local dialects. And a neo writers group is also germinating. Anyway, the fact remains that in the northeast, Hindi journalism has yet to attain more heights.

[8]
Child Literature and Hindi Child Journalism

IN ENTIRE northeast India, apart from Assamese and a couple of regional languages, children literature is not published in any other language. Barring All other languages apart from Manipuri and Assamese are in their developmental stage.

In fact, the first original literature of children was written in Assamese language. Efforts were made to touch the minds of the children through the medium of various folk songs and folk tales, traditionally sung by contemporary poets and storytellers. An attempt was made to provide an interesting literature to children through the folk tales-*'Tejimala'*, *'Chelnirjivekar'*, *'Sadhu'* etc.

The religious and social guru of Assamese society in the 15th –16th century Shankardev and his disciple Madhav Dev though had not authored any child literature but their plays pertinently depict the life and psychology of children characters. Among these vaishnav gurus, - Child form of lord Krishna is bestowed with transcendental qualities in the plays *' Chordhara'*, *'Pinpara Gunchuva'*, *'Arjun Bhanjan'* etc by Madhav Dev and childhood acts of *'Kirtan'* by Vaishnav guru Shankardev. Shirdhar kandli in *'Kankhoa'* and. Ram Saraswati in *'Bhim Charit'* have tried to expose the child psychology pre-eminently.

The fact is that the rise of child journalism in Assam occurred in 1846, after the Christian missionaries in

Shivsagar published a magazine named 'Arunodaya'. Even though this magazine was meant for adult but it also printed various bible stories and stories filled with moral preaching from different countries of the world. The Britishers named Brown, Branson and Cutter published many books- *'Bibler sadhu'* (stories of Bible), *'Shuvani Sadhu'*, *'Sunder Momai'*, *'Mauri Ghowali'*, *'Revar Kahini'*, *'Saru Kaler Dharm', (religion* of childhood), *'Eglur Bah'* , *'Afrikar Konwar'*. (The prince of Africa) etc. At that time Anandram Dhekyal Phukan published- 'Asamia Larar Mitra', a textbook for children. Writer Rasraj Lakhshminath Bejbarua published folk tales impending through ages from grand pa's and grand ma's mouth, in two collections-*'Buddhi Ayer Sadhu'* 1911 and *'Kaka Devta Aru Nati Lara'*. Apart from the above, a book named *'Junuka'* was also published in 1913.

Among the literatures of that period, who did commendable works in the field of development of child literature are writers of textbooks for children use, those were -Padma Nath Gohain Barua and Panindra nath Gogai, writers of poems for children- Anand Chandra Agrawal, Baldev Mahant, Vishay Chandra Viswasi, Dhanai Bara, Md. Suleman khan and composer of other types of child literature - Lambodar Bara, Ratneswar Mahant, Durga Prasad Mazindar Barua and Benudhar Rajkhova are quite imperative.

After being inspired by the principles of Rasraj Bezbaruah, several collections were published in the modern form like- *'Sadhu Katha'* by Vishnu Priya devi, *'Sadhur Bhandal'* by Kumudeshwar Barthakur, *'Sadhu Kathar jolonda'* by Gyananand Bhagwati, *'Assamia Sadhukatha'* by Sharatchand Goswami, *'Sandhiyar Sadhu'* by Trailokeshwari devi Baruani.

In fact, with the beginning of 1929, Assamese child literature found a new direction. Various endowed literature had made successful efforts to enrich the Assamese child literature by their compositions on diverse subjects for children's use. Shri Gagan Chandra Adhikari has written in his article- 'Assamia Bal Sahitya' that a story collection named '*Paribala*' by Dr. Banikant Kakati, '*Maina*' and '*Veer Chatiyar desh*' by Hariprasad Barua, '*Rajasthan Galp*' by Vinand Chandra Barua, '*Jatak mala*' by Dr. Viranchi Kumar Barua, '*Mau Mahabharat*' by Mitradev Mahant, ' *Savitri*' and '*Nal-Damyanti*' by Harendra Nath Sharma were important books composed for children purpose.

Other than those, foreign literatures was also translated few of the prominent ones are- '*Dadair Panja*' by Gyandabhiram Barua, '*Robinson Crooso*' by Benudhar sharma, '*Dabarer Sipare Dhuniya desh*' by Dr. Maheshwar Neog. Similarly, various children purpose books on science and inventions, travelling, biographies and sports were published; among these- '*Latu Mani* ' (Benudhar Sharma), ' *Makhanera Kukura Povali*' (Nabkant Barua)', '*Vigyaner Vismay Batari*' (Dwivendra Nath Sharma)', '*Aadim Yuger Aadim Katha*' (Dr. Bhuwan Mohan Das)', '*Chil Chil Chilla, Bagi Chil Milla*' (Dr Nirmal Prabha Bardolai)', '*Bapuji*' (Mahadev Sharma), '*Akanir Shankardev*' (Premdher Dutt) 'Maniram Divan ' (Chitra Mahant) etc are significant.

In Assamese language several beautiful poems, novels and plays have been written for children among those- ' *Shialar Sing*' (Premdhar Dutt) '*Assamia Omla geet*' ' (Dr. Nirmal Prabha Bardolai), '*Jal Kunwarir Deshat*' (Yogen Sharma), '*Kene Maza*' (Padmedhar Chaliha), ' Phuhar Phen' (Kirtinath Hazarika) etc are important.

The contribution of late Jyoti Prasad Agarawal who was bestowed with multifaceted talent can never be forgotten. Even though he did not write any book on education and child psychology, however he tried to fill the vacuum of children literature in Assamese by his poems and plays for children. *Akman Losh*, '*Akmani Chhovali*', ' *Kumpur Sapon* ' etc are some of the poems written for children by Jyoti prasad.

'*Jyoti Ramayan*' is an incomplete poetic work of late Jyoti prasad. Despite the fact that he had written it for children, yet it is equally valuable for adults as well. '*Jyoti Ramayana*' does not only have the story of *Rama* but also the geographical expanse of

India and its ancient prestige are also incorporated.

Among the plays for children, *'Son Parivali'* and 'Nimati Kaina' are some of the illustrious Jyoti prasad's creations. In fact, Geenabhiram Baruah published *'Lara Bandhu'* from Nagaon in 1886 which is acknowledged as the first Assamese children magazine. But it stopped after the publication of two issues. Same year children magazine named *'Mau'* was published from Guwahati. But it also did not exist for long. After a long time span a magazine named *'Ankan'* was published from Guwahati under the editorship of Hemendra Goswami but it also disappeared in 1918.

Likewise, various magazine for children were published such as *Maina (*1923) edited by Raghunath Chaudhary *Arun* ' from Tejpur edited by Mahadev sharma in 1926, *Amar desh (1931), Por Pakhila* 1931 from Calcutta edited by Harendranath Sharma, *Akan'* (1935), Guwahati edited by Biranchi Kumar Barua ,' *Navjune*' (1937), *'Paarijaat'*, *'Benudhaar*' 1941, edited by Dinanath Sharma from Calcutta, *'Rangdhar*' (1948) edited by Biranchi Barua Guwahati, *Kansijoon' (1948), 'Mangaldai'* edited by Ibrahim Ali, *Deepak (1958), edited* by Lakshayadhar Chaudhary, Guwahati, *Rudali* (1970), *Junbai* (1961), all these publication stopped after some time. Among these *Deepak* was survived the longest period of time. It means that its publication continued from 1958 to 1968. In the same way *Junabai* was published from 1961 till 1970. There is also some information regarding the publication of *'Vismay*' 1969 and ' Manoranjan' children magazine. Presently, following children magazine are being published in Assamese language regularly, These are ' *Safura' 1981,* Guwahati editor Bhavendranath Saikia, *'Mukuta*' (1980), Guwahati editor Kumud Chandra Goswami and ' *Mauchak*' (1975) Johrat editor Shantanu Tamuli. Assam science committee is publishing two magazines based on science subject for children named *'Vigyan Jyoti'* (1961) and *'Avishkaar*'. Among

Assamese Children Newspapers and Magazines

Name of News-papers/Magazine	Year	Editor/ Published by	Place of Publicatn.
Arunodya	1846	Christian missionaries, newspaper contained column for children and also contained bible stories	Shivsagar
Mau	1886	...	Guwahati
Larabandhu (closed after publication of two issues)	1886	Karunabhiram Barua	Guwahati
Akan (published for two years)	1916	Hemchandra Goswami	Nagaon
Maina	1923	Ragunath Chaudhary	Guwahati
Arun	1926	Mahadev Sharma	Tejpur
Amaar desh	1931	...	...
Pakhila	1931	Harendranath Sharma	Kolkata
Akan	1935	Viranchi Kumar Barua	Guwahati
Nayjoon	1937	...	...
Parijaat	1941	Dinanath sharma	Kolkata
Rangghar	1948	Viranchi Kumar Barua	Guwahati
Kanshijoon	1948	Ibrahim Ali	Mongalde
Deepak	1948	L. Chaudhary	Guwahati
Vigyan Jyoti	1961	...	Guwahati
Rudali	1970	...	...
Junbai	1961	...	...
Mauchuk	1975	Shantanu Tomuli	Jorhat
Mukuta	1980	K. C. Goswami	Guwahati
Safura	1981	Dr. B. N. Saikiya	Guwahati
Rajdoot (Only Hindi magazine)	...	Kamleshwar	...
Vismay	1969	...	Guwahati

all these '*Safura*' stands first in terms of circulation and popularity.

There is information about the publication of an only magazine for children named '*Rajdoot*' from Guwahati edited by Kamleshwar. However not much is known about it. Assamese translation of Hindi child magazine '*Chanda Mama*' published from Chennai is also quite popular among children.

Apart from these, the newspaper or magazines published in all these seven states of northeast region necessarily include column for children. In these column, poems, stories and drawing made by the children's themselves are published.

After seeing the Assamese children magazine '*Safura*" *Mauchak*', '*Mukuta*', these cannot be termed as standard magazines because the level of pictures and print is not of good quality. Even the selection of subjects for children's is also not suitable. Assam still holds a scope for a standard children magazine. Chitra mahant who is also a writer of this literature and former secretary of Assam national language publicity committee, informs about the poor condition of literature that-'Once in Kolkata a total ten stories in Assamese were demanded for children between the age group of 9 to 14 but not a single story could not be found. He says that there is an absolute scarcity of agreeable stories in Assamese Language. Presently, Bhaven Nath Saikia editor of ' Safura' has done a fine job on children literature. Apart from him other attempts by Dharmeshwar Katki, Krishnakant Bhattacharaya, Naryana Chandra Das, Surendra Kumar Das, Navkant Barua and others are creditable.

[9]
Assamese Drama and Cinema

ASSAMESE Drama has a firm and strong tradition. The credit for its popularity and dignity could be given to the great, Shri Shankardev and Shri Madhavdev.

The number of plays composed, acted and published in the modern times in Assam have been probably unprecedented. For the ease of studying, Assamese plays could basically be classified into three categories, namely-Mythological plays, historical plays and social plays.

Mythological Drama

'Sitaharan' by Ramakant Chaudhary is the first mythological play of the modern Assamese language. *'Abhimanyu Badh'* (Bharat Chandra Das), *'Savitri- Satyavan'* (Rajnikant Bardolai, Kanak Lal Baruah and Gopal Krishna Deb) *'Harishchandra Upakhyan'* (Purna Kant Sharma),' *Harishchandra'* (Ratneshwer Mahant) and other plays are considered weak form the point of view of drama technique. Among these, the effect of drama acts is visible. In the beginning of 20th century, Chandradhar Barua has composed two mythological plays; these are-'Meghnad Badh' and 'Tilotma Sambhav" Meghanath Badh' has *been acclaimed as* a milestone in the field of Assamese drama. 'Parth Parajay' and 'Bali Badh' written by Durgeshwar Sharma. *'Urvashi Uddhar'* by Dhaniram Dutt, *'Lav-Kush'* by Balram Pathak, *'Shreevats-Chinta'* by Indreshwar Bar

Thakur, 'Bidehi-Vichched' and *'Prachann-Pandav'* by Mitra Dev Mahant, 'Agni Pariksha' By Dandinath Kalita are important creation from point of view of time. Among the mythological dramatist of the of pre- independence period Padma Nath Gohain Baruah is a remarkable dramatist. He has written *'Vanraja'* in a language that is a mixture of prose and poetry. From the point of view of story and technique, Ganesh Gogai's *'Shakunir Pratishodh'* and Jyoti prasad's *'Shonit Kunwari'* are priceless creations.

Atul Chandra Hozarika, who has written a dozen plays in the pre independence period, has also written several mythological and historical plays during the post independence period. Among his creations-*'Nand Dulal'*, *'Beula'*, *'Kurukshetra'*, *'Ramchandra'*, *'Champawati'*, *'Rukminiharan'* *'Savitri'* and others are greatly cherished and much distinguished plays. The influence of Shakespeare is quite noticeable in most of his plays. In his later marks- *'Niryatita Damayanti'* and *'Niryatita Sita'* he has deviated form the earlier influence and has adopted the Indian folk drama style.' *Avsaan'* *'Chitrangda'* and *'Savitri'* by Kamlanand Bhattacharya and *'Visarjan'* and *'Nal Damyanti'* by Anand Chand Barua are acting oriented plays. Several dramas have been written in Assamese by taking prominent characters from *Puranas* as protagonists. Among those, Surendranath Saikia's- 'Karna' and 'Lakshman', Bhavendranath Thakuriya's- 'Maharathi Karna' are worth mentioning. In all these three plays there have been unbeaten attempt to reveal the inner conflict of the characters of Karna and Lakshman.

Among mythological plays, some of the invaluable gift of Assamese Literature are—*'Abhishaptata'* (R.K.Baruah) *'Akal-Bodhan'* (Sharda Baruah) *'Baidehiviyog'* (Mitra Dev Mahant), *'Gurudakshina'* (J. Goswami), *'Kans-Vadh'* (Dambrudhar Hajarika), *'Shri Krishne Janmlila'* (Hem Chandradev Goswami), *'Bhumiputra'* (Narayan Das), *'Amarjivan'* (Ramesh Kalita), *'Tapati'* and *Lopa Mudra'* (G. Barua), *'Nanichor'* (Hiranya Devi), *'Rakshyakumar'*

(Lakshyadhar Chaudhary). In '*Bhumi Putra*' the national feeling of Narakasur is remarkable. In '*Kansa Badh*' and '*Shree Krishner Janmlila*' the influence of the Assamese style of '*Ankiya*' and '*Bhaona*' dramas is quite obvious.

From the playwright and technique standpoint, the mythological Assamese plays are not prosperous enough. Except for –'Milan Tirtha' and other one odd dramas, rest of these are miles apart from the perspective of modern times.

Historical plays

The dramatists of dependent India initiated the process of writing historical drama with a view to whiff the mantra of nationalism. Padamnath Gohai Barua is the father of Assamese historical plays. 'Jaimati' is his first historical play. After this he wrote *Gadadhar', 'Sadhani'* and *'Lachit Barphukan'*. Except for 'Lachit Brafukan, the language of the rest of his plays is poetic and Dialogue are slow and boring and narratives are too long. Other important dramatist of his tradition is Laxminath Bejbarua. He wrote three plays *'Belimar' 'Jayamati'* and *'Chakradhwaj Singh'*. In almost all these three plays, the conflicts of the rulers of Ahom era and the impact of external attacks is depicted. Among the dramatists of pre independence period, Nakul Chandra Bhuyan is a significant play writer *'Baden Barphukan', 'Chandrakant Singh'* and *'Vidrohi- Maran'* are his famous plays. The narratives of his plays are somewhat longer. And there is a lack of co-ordination in the visual-creation. '*Nilamber*' (Prasannalal Chaudhary) is a representative historical novel of the Assamese language. From the standpoint of script, dialogue character depiction purpose and style, it is a unique act-play. Nand and Shachi Patra are two of its live characters. Devchandra Talukdar has written five plays- *'Aassam Pratibha'* 'Haradatt' 'Bamuni Konwar' 'Bhaskar Verma' and 'Radha Rukmini'. Of which, the last three plays are quite successful. His plays generally lack imperative hero and characterization.

Atul Chandra Hazarika is primarily a mythological dramatist and later a historical one. All of his three historical plays –*'Kannuj Kumari'* (1993), *Chhatrapati Shivaji'* (1947) and *'Tikendrajit'* (1959) are his significant contribution to Assamese drama-literature.

In the pre independence period it was not possible to depict a historical heroic character to raise his voice against British policies. This is the reason why most of the dramatist used to consider it their duty to inspire the sentiments of nationalism in all the youth by presenting the patriotism of immortal martyrs who sacrificed their lives for their native land, by raising their voice against the British detrimental policies. *'Maniram Devan'* (Praveen Phukan), *'Piyali Phukan'* (Prafull Baruah), *'Kushal Konwar'* (Surendra Nath Saikia), *'Labhita'* (Jyotiprasad), *'Tikendrajit'* (A.C. Hazarika), '1857' (Yugal Das) and other plays are of the same category. *'Bhogjara'* a play written by actor-dramatist Phani Sharma is a precious gift to the Assamese literature. The internal conflicts and subterfuges of the last Ahom rulers has been portrayed in it. From the point of view of story composition, characterization, dialogue, language and style, it stands as a successful dramatic creation. 'Jerengar Sati', 'Barmanuhar Dola', 'Bararja Phuleshwari (Uttam Barua) are act- plays based on the story of Ahom era. In the first play 'Jayamati's patriotism, her courage and her obeisance for her husband is depicted. In the second play widespread class struggle of Ahom era and futility of feudal classes are presented on an imaginary level. In the third play, hollow ambition of Puleshwari is presented in limited number of scenes. *'Rajdrohi'* Written by Abdul Malik is an acclaimed play based on the story of famous historical person Saturam. In the backdrop of Chinese aggression of 1962, two Assamese plays were written to endorse the feeling of courage, sacrifice, nationalism and martyrdom in our youth, they were - *'Desher Sainik'* (Dhanchandra Das) and *' Juie Pora Sona'* (Phani Talukdar).

Social Plays

In modern era, especially in post-independence period, social plays were composed in more numbers as compared to mythological and historical plays. The social plays, for convenience in its study, can be classified into several groups. For example- Problem based plays, sarcasm based plays, folk plays, symbolic plays, musical plays and propaganda based plays.

Problem based plays

Published in 1857, *'Ram Navmi'*, written by Gunabhiram Barua is the first problem based play. Among the social evils faced by the society at that time, problem of child widow was an important one. Ram- Navmi and Jayanti's suicide presented in the play does not provide any solution but they do force us to think about the evils of child marriage.

In the play 'Kalyani' (Atul Chandra Hazarika), Kalyani is an ideal female character, who being the daughter of a royal priest, dedicates herself to the services of peoples who were called untouchables. From *'Chakai Chakora'* (1937) till now, Satyaprasad Barua has written more than half a dozen problem based plays and has increased the prestige of Assamese drama- literature.

Pravin Phukan has written both historical and problem-based dramas. *'Kal-Parinay', ' Shitikar Ban', 'Assam Hollywood', 'Vishwarupa'* are documents of his dramatic talent.

'Papiatara' (Baldev Saikia), ' *Makrajal*' (Abdul Malik), *'Natun Samaj'* (Ramhari Maral), 'Pratitidan' (Swaraj Nath), 'Kia?' *'Kala Bazar' (Phani* Sharma), *'Nimila Ank'* (Lashaydhar Chaudhary), *'Poorvashri Theatre* (Anil Chandra Thakur), *'Mandand'* (Panchanan Deka), *'Pahila Tarikh'* (Sharda Bardolai), ' *Shilpi'* (Bhadram Saikia), *' Ghat-Pratighat'*, (Anand Kumar), *'Paraajit'* (Dandinath Kalita), ' *Mok Bhot Diyak'* (Medini Kant Thakuriya), *Natun Samaj* '(A.M Bezbaruah), *'Artanad'* (Jiten Bhagwati) etc are some of the important

plays touching the various aspects of economic problems. Economic exploitation, repression, black marketing, dearness etc are fundamental themes of the above-mentioned dramas. *'Ebelar Nat'* (Bina Devi), *'Nimila Ank'*, *'Jeevan Vritta'* etc highlight the economic problem of upper middle and lower middle class.

Modern era sees the problem of communalism increasing day by day. Following plays depict the problem of communalism, such as-*'Sanko'* (Prafulla Bara), *'Jinati'* (Arun Sharma), *'Deshar Mati'* (Medini Thakuriya), *'Sahpathi'* (Md. Sakbul Ali), *'Magribar Ajan'*, (Sharda Bardolai and K. Bhattacharya), *'Urukha Paja'* (Arun Sharma), *'Bhaiyamar Senduria Ali'* (Janardan Thakur), *'Setu'* (Taranath Battacharya) etc. In the plays *'Deshar Mati'*, *'Samadhan'*, *'Uphaar'*, *Badhi'*, *'Janm'*, *'Mok Bhot Diyak'*, *'Mantrir Hukum'*, *'Artanad'*, *' Nanun Purush'* etc, corruption, injustice, exploitation, differences in the word and deeds etc of political leaders are presented.

Sarcasm dominated plays

Many sarcasm based plays have been written in Assamese. Padmanath Gohain Barua's *'Gaobuddha'*, *'Tetan Tamuli'* and *'Bhut Ne Bhram'*, Laxminath Bezbarua's *'Litikai'*, *'Chikar Pati Nikarpati'*, *'Nomal and Panchani'*, Hemchandra Baruas's *'Kania Kirtan'* and *'Bangal-Bangalini'*, Durgaprasad Mazindar Barua's *'Mahari'* and 'Negro' etc are significant sarcastic plays written in initial period. Among the post independence period sarcastic plays- *'Satkar'*, *Kanthrole'* (Prem Narayan), *Bekar Babu* (Tarun Azad Deka), *'Prabhu-Ichar'* (Harish Chandra Bhattacharya), *Esh Deh Dhara* (K.B. Barua), *'Tini Kala'* (Ripunath Budhgohain), 'Kanakata' (S. Barua), *'Apos'*, *'Taqdur'*, *'Pretatmar Paridasshan'* (Surendranath Saikia) etc are important.

Folk Plays

Keeping in view the change in interest, some dramatist diverted from the traditional drama style in their linguistic plays and adopted folk style. An aficionado of Shakespearean style, Atul Chandra Hazarika has adopted this style in two of his plays (Niryatita *Sita, Niryatita Damyanti*). The effect of emotion play is thoroughly evident in *'Kansa- Badh'* (Dambrudhar Hazarika), *'Baidehi Viyog'* (M. Mahant), *'Shri Krishna Janma Lila'* (Hemchandra Dev Goswami) etc. More or less use of folk style can be in the plays- *'Artanad'* (Jiten Bhagwati), *'Janm'* (Mahendra Bara Thakur).

Symbolic Plays

The composition of symbolic plays in Assamese has been done in small form. *'Manir Khela'* written by Bhimshekar Barua, which is a 'Prabodh Chandroday' style play, presents diverse human tendencies and psychological disorders of characters. *'Nemati Kayeena'* written by Jyotiprasad is basically a musical play. The performance of exceptional symbols is found here. *'Janam'* (Mahendra Barthakur), 'Bagh' (Mahendra Barthakur', *'Jeevan-vritta'* (Shri ram Goswami), *'Manush Aru Asur'* (Basant Saikia), *'Jari'* (Vinod) etc are superior plays from the symbolic point of view.

Musical Plays

From the point of view of object and art, Assamese musical plays are still in their adolescent stage. Except for one-odd (*Nemati Kayana, Sonar Sole*) musical plays, rest of them is very weak in terms of subject and style.

Publicity Plays

Advertisement is the main feature of publicity plays and the same is a weak element for the art of drama. *'Setu'* written by Taranath Bhattacharya, *'Lahanda'* by Dev Talukdar, *'Deshar mati'* by Medini Thakuriya, *'Upahaar'* by Sharada Bardolai, *Samadhan'* by Ripunath Budhagohain and *'Sahpathi'* by Md. Makbul Ali are important works.

Assamese Cinema

Assamese film industry has not been as flourishing as the film industries of south India. The production of a film requires huge capital. In addition, it is a highly technical job. Even after being prosperous in terms of natural resources, Assamese people have been lagging behind in terms of economics resources. Many natural and divine calamities, besides the assailments on the border areas have made the Assamese people economically weaker. History is a witness to the fact that British Empire economically exploited Assamese people and the state to a large extent. This is the reason why Assamese literature and education could not develop at a speed that was essential. How was it possible then for the film Industry to thrive?

The credit for producing the first film in the Assamese film industry goes to Jyoti Prasad Agarwal. He produced his first film *'Joymati'* in 1934, in the tea garden of Bholagudi. It was Assam's first talkie movie. Late Aggarwal named his studio - *'Chitra Ban'*. His father did the unofficial inauguration of this studio. Before *Joymati* neither a mute nor a talkie movie was produced in Assam. The first talkie produced in India was Alam- Ara in 1934. Jyomati was India's fourth sound recorded film, which was made in Assamese. The cameraman of this film was Bhopal Shankar Mehta and its sound recording was done by Faizi. At that time, this film was made entirely in the tea garden itself. Tea-leaves were prepared in the day and practice of film acting was done in night in the building of tea factory.

Since then, till today, Assam has come a long way in the area of film-making. Several government film production centers and studios have been constructed where film industry is blossoming. From 1934, till now, many film have been produced in the Assamese languages. Now local Assamese people are also participating in this industry. Late Agrawal took the plot of the story of 'Joymati' from the novel 'Joymati' written by Laxminath Bezbarua, an author of Assamese language. Through the medium of this film he has tried to portray the colourful aspects of the folk-culture, religious rituals, the culture traditions and the attire of people of Assamese society. Even though the film was based on historical subject, the music of the film was taken from Assamese folk songs served as a mirror for life and culture of Assamese people. The story of this very first film is based on the great sacrifice of the princess of Ahom, - Joymati'. This film very successfully shows the breeding and thriving intrigues and conspiracies among the royal progenitors during the Ahom rule. Joymati"s husband - Godhapani is the successor of Ahom dynasty. In order to escape the grasp of the then Ahom ruler, he wanders around from one state to another. Ahom ruling dynasty had a tradition to debar a prince having mark on any organ or abnormality of any organ from ascending the throne. When Ahom spies unable to find the whereabouts of Gorhapani, the king captures Joymati' and severely persecute her so that she may reveal the where bouts of her husband. But that gutsy woman does not speak out anything about her husband. Even when her husband in disguise comes and asks her to tell his where about, but the dauntless lady does not divulge the location of her husband and lastly succumbs to the tortures and dies. The film ends with the death of Joymati'.

The purpose of Jyoti prasad was to show a true and an important incident from Assamese history, keeping the custom, song- music-dance of Assamese society in the backdrop of the story.

The first screening of Joymati' was done on 10th of March 1935, at Raunaq Mahal Theatre of Kolkata. Then his film was screened at Kumar Bhaskar Natya Mandir on 20th March apart from this he also produced three other films- '*Indra Malati*', '*Amar Gaon*', and '*Maan ke Kal ki Agney Dhune*. He wanted to make two more films but died and his dreams were left unfulfilled.

Jyoti Prasad Aggrawal : Multifaceted talent

Jyoti Prasad was born on 17th June 1903, in the Dibrugharh town of upper Assam. He was born during the seventh month of his mother's pregnancy. He was very thin but astrologer had predicted that this child would enlighten his own name and his family's name. But at that time no body could imagine that this child born in the seventh month will illuminate not only his descent but also his country. Kiranbala Devi was his mother who belonged to the famous Tiru Kakti family from Balaghat Shiv sagar district of upper

Jyotiprasad Agrawal

Paramanad Assam region. His father's name was Aggrawal. He had great interest in the literary activities and had infinite respect for Gandhi ji. The ideals of his father affected the son as well. His interest in music, nationalist ideals and literary activities had its total effect on Jyoti prasad. In 1918, he along his father Paramanad Aggrawal participated in the Ahmedabad session of the congress. The speeches of Gandhi ji and other national leaders had a positive effect on his adolescent mind. In 1927, when Gandhi ji came to visit Assam he stayed along with the Aggarwal family at Tejpur. Here Jyoti prasad got the opportunity to stay in close proximity of Gandhiji. He felt great pleasure in serving the Mahatma and he became his fan.

Jyotiprasad had spent his childhood days in an environment with an abundance of nationalism, literature and music. In his adolescent days, he got the companionship and guidance of Laxmidhar Sharma, Amiya Kumar Das and some other student leaders. In 1919, when he was just 16, he was given his first duty of a responsible public work. He wrote his first Assamese drama 'Shonit kunwari' at the age of 14 because of the literary atmosphere that was prevailing in his house. Jyotiprasad took his primary education from Tejpur high school, Dibrugarh government school and Dibrugarh George Institute. He passed the ninth class examination in 1921 but was not allowed to sit in the matriculation examination because of low age group. After that he took a decision that he will not study in government school and took admission in a school named *'Godia Sarva Vidyatan'* in Kolkata managed by Deshbandhu Chittaranjan Das. This school was established for those people who were declared unfit for admission to government school because of their participation in noncooperation movement.

Jyoti Prasad Aggarwal

He passed his matriculation examination from here and took admission in National College at Kolkata. Great nationalist leader Shubhas Chandra Bose was the principal of the college. He studied here up to second year of intermediate. After the closure of the national college, though his education stopped but his desire for higher education never diminished. In 1929, he went to England for higher education and also appeared in the examination o Edinburgh University but could not pass the examination. He again appeared in the examination for second time and he was allowed to study on some terms and conditions. He took admission in M.A.; his subjects were -Economics, law, Sanskrit and Philosophy but he could not study further after one session. In England itself he studied British Drama Treatise and then travelled to western countries. He met Himanshu Ray in Germany who was a famous personality of Indian film industry. He spent seven months in Germany in the proximity of Himanshu Roy and became versed with the practical and theoretical aspect of film-making. He consulted Sri Roy with great intent, about film making in India and its professional utility. Jyoti Prasad returned to India in 1930. He returned to India with firm desire of making film in Assamese language. Accordingly he started the work of film-making. He produced his first film in Assamesse language- 'Joymati". He had to struggle a lot while the making of this film. He had to face great difficulty, mainly because of the female character,

After coming back from England, he married on his own volition, Devjani, daughter of Khageshwar Bhuyanni of Khalahabhari of Dibrugarh district; she at that time was a student of local high school. After marriage Devjani left her studies and started helping her husband in his works. They had two sons and five daughters. Later on, one of their sons died at a tender age. Even his wife Devjani died prematurely. His brothers extended their full support in looking after his children. His children grew up to become proficient and of good disposition following the aptitude, morals and temperament of their father.

Jyotiprasad's father was a proficient literature, literature-fan, music connoisseur and a political personality. All these three qualities came down to

Jyotiprasad. At the age of fourteen, he composed a play that was quite successful in theatres. The name of play was '*Shonit kunwari*'. Its story was mythological. A successful attempt was made in this play to highlight the relation ship between the grandson of Shri Krishna- Anirudha and Usha, daughter of Shonitpur (Now Tejpur) king.

After that he never looked back in the field of literature and composed various plays, poems, biographies, short stories etc. Some of his compositions are :-

Plays- *'Shonit Kunwari' (1926) 'Karengar Ligiri', (1937), 'Rupalim' (1960), 'Labhita' (1948), 'Nimati Koina, (1964), 'Sonpakhili' (1964) and 'Khanikar' (1977)*

Poems- *'Luitar paraar Agnisur' (1979), 'Jyoti Ramayana (uncompleted)*

Biographies - *'Chandra Kumar Aggrawal'*

Short stories- *'Jyoti Satsori' (1967), ' Sameleno Mein Bhashan'. 'Assamiya Sangetar Rupa' (1936), 'Naturn Dinar Kristi' (1947), ' Pohara Loi (1947), 'Silpir Prithivi', ' Adiur Janki Baat' (1949).*

Essays- *'Jyotirdhara'* (1969)

Music- Jyoti prasad Aggrawal was a lyricist and musician of excellent category, the skill he inherited from his ancestors. In his songs, he gave main importance to the '*Bargeet*', 'Bangeet', ' Bihugeet', 'Ainam', 'Biyanam', 'Hasorigeet', and other such folks songs, religious songs, milkman's songs, wedding songs etc. He also composed assorted musical tunes for these songs so that they become melodious and pleasing to the ear. He named them 'Kamrupi Raga'. Presence of dramatic element and momentum, were the reasons for the popularity of his songs. As far as the instruments are concerned, he made full use of drum, flow and string instruments along with western musical instruments without any hindrance.

His songs were utilized greatly during the period of independence struggle. His songs of national renovation stirred up the masses and gave a message of national awakening. Through the medium of his songs, he gave the message of harmony and love to people of different religious groups and beliefs. A message of brotherhood and mutual accord was spread. In his songs, he said that the Assamese culture is a part of Indian culture. Jyotiprasad was cited with-*'Gana'* or *'Gana Shilpi'* meaning-'the artist of the masses'. He composed his music for people of all kinds.

He composed songs enriched with the sentiments of nationalism besides he also composed love songs. His song present a picture of hope and despair of diligent Indian farmers, labourers draining out their sweat and blood, and people struggling to civilize their lifestyle in spite of all the difficulties. Following lines of the poem are worth attention-

Keep special qualities in tact
Of your precious civilized life
But still be friends to each other
This is a unity song of the new world humanity
This way I write the religious text
This will be the ideal of this life
All are children of human beings
Today come and be one
Say the only song
Sing the only song
Unity of mind, unity of purpose
And become one in life

The same sentiments are reflected in the following poems :-

I am a Hindu
I am a Muslim
I am a young man of new generation.
My god is in temple and Mosque
My god is present in every named house
He is in my heart and outside
My lord is in rivers and in forest
In the sky and even above that...

Nowhere can one find a better example of his secular viewpoint. He cautioned the people to be careful concerning those people who desired to annihilate the harmony among

Hindus and Muslims as well as among tribals and non-tribals.

He deemed music and fine arts as an inseparable part of each other. In his view, a fine art was the greatest wealth and invaluable treasure of human life. He had strong faith toward the cultural mindset of the people. While expressing his views regarding Shreemant Shankardev he wrote-Shankardev tried to reach civilization and culture to the people and he had been absolutely successful in that. This is the reason why Assamese people possess an esteemed and affluent refined culture. We cannot imagine a cultural development without the people.

Thus, Jyotiprasad gave a memorable contribution by-giving a message of upliftment of the nation, unity, love, brotherhood in his services towards literature as well as by expressing literary view points about the preservation of our culture.

Political View point

Jyotiprasad got a political lineage from his ancestral heritage. His father himself was a liberal politician. He was completely overpowered by the view of Gandhi ji. As told earlier, in his childhood itself he went to Ahmedabad along with his father to participate in the session of Indian National Congress. He was impressed with the speech of Gandhi ji. Later Gandhi ji stayed at his house during his Assam visit and he got the proximity of Gandhi ji from close quarters.

Since he was impressed with Gandhi ji at a very tender age (16) he had to take over the chairman ship of the cultural wing of Assamese student Association.

On the call of Gandhi ji in 1921, he participated in the noncooperation movement. He founded an association and set up a center in Gamiri to provide speed and direction for this work. He collected money for Tilak Swaraj Fund; for which he had to visit several villages. In 1926, when he was in London at the time congress session, even from there he sent to his bother, a song packed with the sentiments of nationalism, which was later sung during the session.

In 1931, he constituted a children volunteer force with the purpose of inculcating among children, feeling of love towards their native land,, so that they become a capable citizen of India. So that they could be on their own to work for the freedom struggle. A teenage girl named kanak lata was also member of this youth squad; she joined it in 1931 and received training from Jyotiprasad Aggarawal. In 1942, when quit India movement was on its extreme, Kanak lata (name of the child) led a march from Shonitpur. She demonstrated great courage and dexterity and unfurled the tricolor at Gohpur police station despite immense resistance from the armed policeman and preserved the prestige of the '*Vaner Sena*' of Jyotiprasad Aggarwal. Even the 'lathi charge' of police men could not deter her from fulfilling moral purpose of Kanak lata. She succeeded in unfurling the flag but she was shot and she died on the spot.

Personality

He was a lover of discipline and active person. Among the freedom fighters of the freedom struggle period, he considered Gandhi ji as the greatest leader. He was always in favour of association of lower classes. During the constitution of a volunteer squad when he was travelling to different villages the police arrested him. The court penalized him a rigorous imprisonment of 15 months and a fine of five hundred rupees. When he was not able to pay the fine, the imprisonment was extended for another six month. While he was serving his jail term, he became seriously ill. The officers released him so that he could receive proper care.

Meanwhile, he involved himself in film production, in order to fulfil his life long desire but immediately after the completion of the film he again jumped into politics in 1936. His role in the 1942 movement was commendable. But he never participated in the upheavals in the violent form. He travelled Assam extensively and spread the mantras of revival among the people; because of which he came in the eye of British government and he had to remain underground for some time. Even while being underground, he was in constant touch with the congress leaders and acted according to the discussion he had with them.

He also fought against those leaders who kept their self-interest above the interest of the nation and put the national interest at stake. He motivated such selfish leaders and cautioned them :-

O you who have became blind
From self interest, wealth and power
You, who have worn a mask,
Of serving the people
People now are aware of you
Be ware! Beware

In another poem he wrote :-

You do not know
People whom you think
Uneducated, foolish and uncivilized
Over whom you want to rule
As a self-styled leaders
They have now awakened completely
They have understood their duties and responsibilities.

Jyotiprasad was also an expert in architecture and painting and he used them with abundance, in his compositions. In drama works and even in the construction of a stage for his film 'Joymati", he used architecture and drawing quite skilfully. The way he described state of Ahom dynasty and its opulence in his first drama work it, clearly signifies that he had adequate knowledge of architecture.

In the history Assamese cine world, another shining name arrives. This great personality is Bhupen Hazarika. Like Jyoti passed Agrawal, Bhupen da is also blessed with multifaceted talent and is a leading protagonist in the field of education, literature, politics music etc. Only difference between the two is, that one gave recognition to Assam before the independence of India and the other urbanized the vanity, culture, and vitality of Assam in the whole world after the Independence of India.

Dr. Bhupen Hazarika : A Brief Introduction

Dr. Bhupen Hazarika was born in the year 1926 in a place named Sadia in Assam. He was born in a very poor family. Bhupen's father was an ordinary teacher in a school.

Dr. Bhupen Hazarika

Later On, he was promoted to be a magistrate. At that time Hazarika was a quite young. While the time of his rise Hazarika's father retired on a meagre pension of rupees hundred and forty five, which was insufficient for his schooling and education. Nevertheless, of his interest in education, led him to succeed in his endeavours. He managed to obtain a post graduate degree in Political Science from Banaras Hindu university. Even after that the struggle kept following his life and in pursuit of Some solution, he visited America. By chance or by sheer coincidence, he met a gentle man and a great Negro singer, named Paul Robson. He enlightened him with the fact that songs can be successfully used as the medium for social-change. Bhupen Hazarika was primarily interested in songs only. After coming here he saw that microphone and movie camera would be the strongest medium of expression, in the present and coming century. For PhD, the subject he opted was- 'the role of mass communication in public education in the India of future'. After returning from there, Bhupen hazarika had to sing for his living. Poverty-stricken that he was had to earn money to buy films. Although when Jyoti prasad Aggarwal had begun film-making he was the owner of two tea gardens. However, he had on his heads the burden of upbringing and educating nine children The destitution became an inspiration in Bhupen progression. He had boundless aptitude and a desire of the quality of grasping. Gradually, he touched higher horizons in his field of work and never looked behind. He has worked in more than 450 Assamese, Bangla and Hindi films as director, musician and lyricist. He has produced many films. His important films are-*'Era Batar Sur' (1956), ' Shakuntala' (1961), 'Pratidhvani' (1967), 'Loti- Ghoti' (1967), 'Chik-Mik-Bijury' (1969), 'Man Prajapati' (1978), 'Svikarokti' (1986), 'Siraj' (1988), 'Chameli memsaab' (1975), 'Ek pal' (1986), 'Rudali' (1983) serial –'Lohit Kinare'.*

Dr. Bhupen Hazarika has received the national award for the best film direction for his films *'Shakuntala', 'Pratidhvani'* and *'Loti Ghoti'*. He was adorned with 'Padamshree award in 1977 and with *Sangeet Natak* academy award in 1987. In 1992, he was festooned with highest award of film world- 'Dada Sahab Phalke award'.

Bhupen da is a proficient director, musician and lyrics besides he is also prosperous with literary talent. He has also edited the Assamese literary magazine' Amar Pratinidhi' published from Kolkata. For his literary talent, he was elected as the president of Assam Sahitya Sabha in 1993.

Bhupen da was perturbed with the neglect of Assam. Jyotiprasad Aggrawal was also a Dada Sahab Phalke of

Assam. From then on, till now the Assamese film industry is passing through phase of struggle. Many great national personalities visited Assam, many Hindi film producers keep coming, Hindi films are distributed here, but the screening of Assamese film does not take place. Anguished by such prejudiced treatment, Bhupen da fought and won an election in 1967, as an independent candidate, against the congress, on the issue of construction of a film studio in Assam and waiving off of the entertainment tax of films for one year. After coming to power he contributed towards the establishment of Jyoti *Chitraban'*, got a small studio constructed and also started a custom of returning the entertainment tax which was later on accepted by different state of India. This contribution helped a great deal in the production of Assamese film and also commenced the production of various Assamese films.

In 1935, he quit professorship and went to Kolkata with an aim of making Assamese film and composing lyrics and music. He associated himself with the Satyajit Ray led movement in 1956 and was also active in the constitution of film society. Film society was also constituted in Assam. Here he used to regularly bring great talent from film world such as Satyajeet Ray, Mrinal Sen, Gulazar so that an environment conducive for the making of excellent films is created in Assam.

In fact, Bhupen Da is basically a lyricist. He aimed though that at film should serve as the conveyor of his music. He was not in favour of making historical films. He preferred musical films and desired to communicate with the viewer in the language of his songs. He considered entertainment as the main issue for making films. Awards have no meaning for Dr. Hazarika, who is bestowed with multifaceted talent and bedecked with many awards. Therefore, when it was announced that he will be awarded with the highest of film world in 1992, then his humble reaction was - it is not merely an a honour for me but for the whole of north east India. Such an 'India' is honoured which has always been subjected to negligence.

This is also true that he has been honoured not only for his works related to Assamese, Bangla, and Hindi films, but for his attachment and commitment in keeping alive the spirit of Indian culture in films through the medium of his lyrics and music. Bhupen Da's songs, music and films provide a glimpse of Indian folk culture. His music holds the pain of a common man. I spoke to him during the Dada Sahab Phalke award ceremony.

Q. Bhupen Da- you are a multifaceted personality. Can one say that rather then you being honoured with the 'Dada Sahab Phalke' the award itself has got honoured..?

A. No, I do not think so. I am not so contemptuous. This is quite a prestigious award and it is definitely greater than me. I am fortunate to have received it. I believe it to be the honour of the whole of Northeast. Jyoti prasad had started the process of film making in Assam in 1933. No one had received such a great honour in all these years and so people felt neglected. After this award , there has been a diffusion of self-esteem in peoples associated with Manipur, Bodo, Arunachali films. They are filled with excessive joy.

Q. You had once said that you consider your music as a means of social change? Will you explain it somewhat?

A. I have always considered my music/ song as a weapon for social change. Real songs are those which portray justice in magnified form belittle injustice. A Song should be a song. It should not be slogan. When I was M.L.A, then I had used my 'Gan' (songs) as a 'Gun' against the party in power. Whenever I come across an incident of murder, kidnapping in northeast, my soul disconsolate with all these. Some time I feel that I should throw the pen. Sometime I wonder where has the moral value of society gone, why is this happening? Now there is need to do something. So that old moral value of the society make a come back. I am not depressed with the present situation, I am an optimist and I think that old values will return and will certainly return.

Q. You are also the chairmen of largest literary organization of Assam i.e. '*Assam Sahitya Sabha*' apart from that you are also active in the field of music lyrics and film. How come you are able to do all these things at a time?

A. To accomplish all these works I generally sleep only 2 to 3 hours daily. Apart from that youngsters also help me. I take my work as a challenge. Perhaps people are not able to assume my age after seeing my involvement in so many jobs at the same time. Some people say that my age is 40 or 45, but the fact is that I am 67 years old. I am not a chief minister who will ensemble all the pleasure and comforts for all his works. I am not much resourceful to appoint somebody for these jobs. All these work have to be done by, me. All these awards also increase my enthusiasm. I will say... *Tair–tair raha hoon,man majhdhaar kitne hi kitne sagar....* ('I am swimming but middle of my mind has so many oceans)?

Q. As the discussion has traverse towards 'Rudali' I want to ask one or two question about this first of all - 'Rudali' has a presence of Rajasthani folk culture and music. You must not be knowing much about there but then how did you create a tune so good?

A. No! No! Right from childhood I had been researching on various music and after that only I evolved as 'Bhupen Hazarika'. Right from my childhood days I have travelled through the country. I felt that

Rajasthani folk music is quite advanced. In 'Rudali' we have developed a creative tune by playing rajasthani musical instrument in the rajasthani style. Take a scene from this film- when there is a rainfall in the desert after many years. Just imagine about the music at the time of rainfall and feel the life. To feel both in concert is a unique experience in itself. Usually people has portrayed desert as a blank but we have shown life in it. 'Shanichari' (Dimple Kapadia) is dry like a desert but even she has a flavour, affection and audacity and courage to reject the enticement of Zamindar (the landlord). We have demonstrated the beauty of her mind, or song or a word, through the medium of music.

Q. What were the musical instrument you have used in this film?

A. Purely Indian instruments. Rajasthani lute (having four strings), miniature bells (Ghungroo) hanging in the camel neck , Indian mandolin, tambourine, and rest of the jing-ling words such as word of storm, or humming tone of water etc. have been taken.

Q. Was it difficult to give words to all these music?

A. We did not have to work hard , but had to research certainly. That is why it took two years for the completion of this film. What happens in today's Hindi films? When I ask him what do they want, film director come and say- Dada! Give two sad songs, two half sad songs. Now tell me, isn't it absurd. Then I tell them that I do not know music of this kind.

Q. Who is the best male and female singer in your opinion?

A. It is very difficult to opine this. How can we say that Lata is better or Asha. In some of the songs Lata is good but in some Asha is equally good. In' Chameli

Mem Sahaab' I had asked class 9th student 'Kavita Krishana Murti' to sing and she got president award for the same. Then how came we say that Kavita is better than Lata or Lata is better then Kavita. Please do not compare but certainly Lata is still a genius.

Q. **'Assamese films are dying and they are being replaced by commercial Hindi film presently what are you doing to provide a respectful place to other regional films of Assam or northeastern region?**

A. Yes, something has to be done. If Assamese films have to survive than some producers have to sacrifice themselves. Only then success will come in hand. Government should also see to it that regional films are given encouragement as against of Hindi films in this region. The beauty of regional films is something unique. Government should act on making on community halls and on film policies and producers should be given necessary economic security.

[10]
Son of India : Gopinath Bardolai

FREEDOM fighter, follower and supporter of Gandhism, worshipper of truth and sacrifice, the name of Gopinath Bardolai is etched in the history of Assam.

Gopinath Bardolai

A great visionary and torchbearer of the political and Social movement of Assam, the distinguished Bardolai

Shri Gopinath Bardolai

became the first administrator i.e. Prime Minister (Chief Minister) of Assam in independent India. Having drawn inspiration from Gandhism during the struggle for independence, he dedicated his entire life to the boycott of imported clothes, spinning Yarn, propagating a khadi and eradication of toxic drugs like opium from Assam. Despite being tortured several times during his term of imprisonment, Bardolai's noble resolve remained undeterred.

Gifted with a farsighted personality, he led the freedom struggle with extreme smoothness. During his chief Minister ship in 1947, he bravely opposed the congress proposal of giving shelter to fifty thousand refugees by saying-he can leave the post of Chief Minister but can not put the load of refugees on Assam. He proposed and executed a plan for local landless people by properly arranging and distributing the cultivable land in Assam.

During his administration he made special effort for industrial development of Assam and also planned to set up easy to establish industries based on the raw materials available in Assam such as Jute, Plywood and paper industry.

Biography

Lokpriya Gopinath Bardolai was born on 6th June 1890 in the Raha village of Nagaon district. His father's name was Buddhishwar Bardolai. His Mother Praneshwari Devi died when he was just twelve year old. His sister Shashikala acted as his guardian. He obtained the title of B.L. from Calcutta University in 1917. He was first appointed as a headmaster of Sonaram High School Guwahati. In 1918 he married Surbala, the daughter of Bhumikant Majinder Barua, a native of Guwahati. He had total eleven children.

He started to work as a lawyer in 1918. In 1921, he participated in noncooperation movement launched by Mahatma Gandhi and left the profession of Lawyer. He spent three days in imprisonment. He became Joint Secretary in the Pandu Session of the Congress in 1934. In 1934, he became the Chairman of Guwahati Municipal Council. This year itself he got an opportunity to come in close proximity with Mahatma Gandhi. Gandhi ji selected him as the first person for Civil disobedience. He was arrested on 11th December 1940 AD and was sent in imprisonment for one year. In 1937, when the World War-II began, he resigned from the cabinet after being in power for Thirteen Months. He was again arrested in 1942 and was sent to Jorlat Prison. In 1946, he was elected as the congress nominee for the legislative assembly and was made Chief Minister (then Prime Minister).

Developmental Scheme and achievements of Bardolai Cabinet

The foundation of Guwahati University, Assam Engineering College, Assam Ayurvedic College, Committee for the propagation of National Language, Assam Medical College, Dibrugarh, Kamrup Academy, B. Barua College, Assam State museum, Saraniya Kastrurba Ashram, Mauman Ashram in Boko and expansion of the Lakhimpur railway line from Tejpur were completed after his death. Various plans that were executed were Guwahati high court, Agricultural University, Police training college, Forest Training College, Co-operative Training College, Compulsory primary education, opium prohibitory law 1947. The success of opium prohibition in Assam is one of the creative planning of Gandhi ji. "Literary contribution of Bardolai"

Many books written by him were published. *'Shree Ram Chandra', Uddhadev', 'Yishu', 'Khisht', 'Hazrat Mohammed', 'Gandhii ji', 'Tarun ram Phukan', 'Anasakti Yog'* etc are counted as unusual compositions.

About Shree Gopinath Bardolai, Shree Kedar Mal Brahman (who was an M.L.A at that time) has opined " He was popular, admired in the country, justice loving, true nationalist, compassionate for the poor and Savior of tribals. Perhaps a great leader like him will never be born again in

Assam. He had no lust for power. When he was made the Chief Minister (at that time prime minister) he objected. He desired to serve the country independently. We, the member of legislative assembly forced him to become a Chief Minister".

Shree Brahman further says "Several important institutions such as University, high court, Assam museum, Ayurvedic college, Veterinary hospital etc were established by the concerted efforts of Late Bardolai. Without his endeavors perhaps Assam would have been left behind".

During the tenure of Shree Bardolai, another member of legislative assembly- Gauri Shankar Bhattacharya in his oenology has said-I remember it quite Vividly that even though he was a lawyer, his attention was more on social work and less on his occupation. He did not appreciate any discrimination among people.

The greatest testimony of him being against any cast discrimination was that -his personal servant was a Schedule Cast person (*Harijan*). Bardolai Ji used to have his meals and water served by him. It was by his efforts only, the *Harijans* of Cheni Kuthi could be resettled in Marakhali and Ambari Harizans colonies.

[11]
Tribal Dances of Assam

ASSAM is the confluence of various cultural forms and styles. According to a belief, the Assamese dance traditions rate as the oldest in India. A quick scan of the history of Assam supports its vintage. However, any authentic information on the long-standing and rich traditions of the period prior to the Ahom rule has not yet been obtained.

In the *'Natya Shastra'* of India, there is certainly some reference of a particular dance form in 'Pragjyotishpur'. In the Historical documents, statues, texts (i.e. *Kalika Purana and Yogini Tantra*) one gets some information about Music, Instruments and dances, however it is not sufficient. In the *'Abhinay Darpan'*, of Nandikeshwar, Usha, Daughter of Banasur, has been shown in the *'Nritya Mudra'* (dance pose) of *Natraja.*

Shiva

In the 7th century, great Chinese traveller HuanTsang came for the first time during the tenure of the rule king Bhaskar Burman of Kamrup. It is said that during his month long stay he enjoyed, each day, the dances & music of this place. Till of late, various Temples i.e. Parihareshwar, Hajo, Vishwanath Dergaon etc had the tradition of Dances as the mode of prayers. Once in a year, Kamakhya Temple still has the custom of presenting "Devadhani" and Devdha dances in front of Snake god-*Manas.*

Amongst the Assamese Dances *'Ojapalli'* is the oldest (*Oja*-Music & dance group leader & *pali*-group), in fact this dance is performed to offer prayer to Snake God M*anas*. Later on this dance was included within Ramayana and Mahabharata during the Nav Vaishnav movement (during Shri Shankar dev's period). And it got its popular name - *'Biyaher Oja'*. In Mangaldai, within the Kamroop & Darang district, the *Ojapalli* dance is fairly popular.

Devdhani Dance

This also comes within the worship of Snake God. In Devdhani dance, the performer has to be an unwed female and she is supposed to be dedicated towards Devi Padma. While dancing it is required that her hair are open and her attire is like a woman soldier. In this type of dance the dancer keeps dancing to the beats of a huge Drum *"Jaidhol"* till she falls unconscious, later on when she regains consciousness; she resumes singing the last part of the song, which describes how Behula rescued and brought back the life of Lakhindra.

Satriya Dance

Founded by Shri Shankardev, Shri Madhevdev & Shri Damoder Dev, *Satriya* Dance school is a recognized Classical dance Institute within this dance form, there are two kinds of dances -Nritya & Nritta.

Nritta includes gesticulation of body parts and dramatic feeling. *Chali, Jhumura Nadu-, Bhangi, Natua, Baha* and other dance forms come within "Nritta" Style of Dancing. And in the *Nritya* Dance each moment and every *Bhav* (feeling) has a meaning of its own. It has three main *Gharanas*- Kamalbari Mudra, Dakhinpat Mudra, and more or less all other Satria Mudras. Most of the Satriya Dances are tough in nature and mainly are meant for the males only. This is the reason why females are not permitted to participate in Satriya dance. Till recently, Purohits only, patronized this dance form but now the females are also accepting this dance.

In fact, Assam is the assimilation of various tribes. People from various outside places came and brought along several varying cultures, whichever first tribes came to settle could not preserve its original culture.

This is the reason behind the change in the new dance style from the original one. Unlike the other folk dances of the world, the dances of Assam are not only the expressions of Joy but also a means to display during religious ceremonies. Almost in all the tribal communities the Bihu dance has a common dance style.

Bodo Dance

Within the Indo-Mongol community, Bodo Community has an outstanding cultural tradition. These tribals present the historical stories through the medium of various folk dances and Music. The majority of these tribals are found in Gwalpara and Darang districts. The folk dances of Bodo tribes are fine and stand perfect on the scientific scale. Their dances can be categorized into four groups- *Kherai, Habajnai, Bagarumba and Baisakhu* "*Kherai* dance is associated with the worship of Gods & Goddesses. "*Habajnai* is associated with wedding ceremonies-"*Begarumba* dances" find the place during festive occasion or during the humorous moments among women, where as *Baisakhu* is associated with harvest season or New year celebrations. Dancers dance by moving their steps forward and backward and also match then to the tunes and Rhythm of the music.

The most scientific and attractive of the dances of the Bodo Tribes is the "*Bagarumba* Dance". While dancing the dancers spread the hand woven colourful cloth from both ends between hand and neck. It gives the view of flying butterflies.

Missing or Miri Dance

Missing or Miri Tribes are also quiet primitive tribes of upper Assam. These tribes are related to Mongolian Tribes, those settled along the Subansiri, Siyang, Dishang & other rivers and later on spread to other areas. Farming & weaving were the two of their primitive professions. Main Dances of these tribes are-*'Cheloya', Mibu, Chipak, Aarik, Ali-e-Liyang, Aarik-Inam, Kaban, O-U-Upnam and Ai-Nitam.* These tribes, living on the hills would dance while coming down towards the plain areas. These dances were known as *'Cheloya'*.

The life struggle was depicted in *Aarik-inam*, while Harvesting- *Ali-e-Liyang, O-U-Upnaam* during Hunting, *Mibu* dance to please Gods & Goddesses and the Young boys and girls indulge in the *Ai-Nitaam* Dance.

Karbi Dance

Karbi tribes are found in the Karbi Anglang districts. However some of these tribes are also spread towards Nagaon, Kamrup, and in the hills of North Kachhar. There is no information regarding the origin of this tribe. Historians are of the opinion that these people came from South East Asia. It is interesting to note that they do not claim to be having any sort of relations with any of the Assamese tribal communities. Farming, fishing and hunting are their means of living. They have been recognized on the most primitive natives of Assam.

The dances these tribes are limited in numbers. In the cremation ceremony *'Chomana Kaan'* dance is performed,

Rabha Dance

while dancing '*Chong-Ka*'style people stand in a circle and hold hands. Young girls and boys hold the Coats and belts of each other respectively while dancing. In addition, the tradition of dancing during fishing, hunting & farming, is a recent development.

Dimacha-Kachhari, Kuki & Jemi Naga tribes living in North Kochhar hills too have various colourful Folk Dances.

Rabha Dance

Amongst few of the important plain area-tribes of Assam, Rabha people too have the tradition of folk dances during festivals & religious occasions.

'*Chathar*' dance, is performed during spring season while the worship of '*Baikhu*. These tribes have dances for hunting & fishing times.

'*Bou* dance of '*Kachar*', '*Fakail*' of Jaipur, *Bihu* of Moran community, 'D*evri*' of North Lakhimpur are also some of attractive dance forms.

'*Kushan*' dance is very popular among the people of Gwalpara. '*Bance*' Dance is a group dance, in which a Group of people perform with pieces of Bamboos in their hands. The upper side of the piece is decorated with the bunches of hair. This dance is prevalent among 'Rabhas and Muslims. The other popular dances of this district are – *Kati* Dance, *Hudum* Dance and *Biya* (wedding) dance.

Bihu Dance

Bihu is the National festival of Assam, which is celebrated during spring season or on the arrival of New Year. It is celebrated during the make up ceremony of mother earth. Bihu dance is performed to celebrate this festival. On the eve of '*Chaitra Sankranti*' the groups of all, young & old go door to door to greet and wish New Year blessing to the neighbours & relatives. *Husuri* is sung before Bihu Dance. After which the young men stand in a line. The dance is performed till the guests are pleased enough. This goes on for 7 days. The ancient tradition of Girls dancing Bihu in Jungles is not prevalent any more.

As the Civilization developed, Hindu dances too saw changes and now it is confined till the stage only. Currently Yong men & women in Assam perform the Bihu Dance during joys and festivity. There is no comparison to the attraction of Bihu Dance in the field of Music & Rhythm. The beats compel even bystanders to start moving his/her steps. '*Dhola* and *Pepa*' (made of buffalo horns) are the musical instruments used especially for the dance. Apart from the aforesaid dances, there are many other kinds of dances. But due to lack of adequate information in this regard, the dances of the remote areas could not be mentioned here. Any ways, Assam is the confluence of various dances, which is the perfect example of unity in diversity.

[12]
Where Every Woman is A Weaver!

WHEN visiting Assam, one is surprised by the presence of a weaver's loom in every house in most villages. You would find the women of the house spinning yarn to meet domestic or commercial needs.

In many states of India the profession of fishing or weaving is considered a second grade job restricted to people

Weaving on Weavers loom

of some select community. But Assam has no such distinction and without a thought of cast, religion, and social status, weaving is taken up by all and almost every house has a weaving loom. Knowledge of weaving in considered an essential part of a girl's education.

Here weaving clothes or manufacturing is considered the work of creative art. Be it a plain region or hills, every place would find women indulged in weaving clothes. From a Queen to slave women, from *Gosains*, Brahman to *'Kevats'* the women of all community weave clothes. Once during his stay in Assam Gandhiji had said- 'Each woman of Assam is a born weaver'.... They create folk tales in the clothes. The women of Assam are expert is the art of weaving. I have started admiring them even more since I have come to know about this fact. Although being weavers, keeping the beauty and the covering quantity intact, they have practised prudence *(Mitvyata)* in their outfits'.

Assamese weavers loom Industry is actually 200 years old. For the villagers this has always been a part of elite life style, since ages. This is the biggest amongst the small scale Industries of Assam. Around 8 lakhs people are involved in the same. For the natives of Assam, it comes under the full time or part time or the leisure time job. Weaving Industry is the main source of its economical constitution; more so it also serves a medium of employment for village people.

Mostly all the tribes of the state weave the clothes with various colourful and attractive patterns and interesting colour combinations and contrasts. Around 30 KM away from Guwahati is an area 'Sualkuchi, where every house weave clothes on traditional and modern patterns with trade's point of view, and that is why its also known as 'Manchester of Asia'.

Assamese women have a typical style of dressing. They wear *'Mekhla'* (Knee length skirts) *Riha* (Sheet covering chest) and a *'Shawl'*. The red embroidered border of *Riha* looks attractive and is suppose to be symbolic. *'Munga'* is the usual outfit of females. During winters men prefer to wear long sheet of white silk. Normally Assamese women do not wear *Riha* but it is mandatory to wear *Riha* on her wedding. With the help of various geometric structures and colourful pattern of flowers etc. people make *Mekhla, Riha, Chader Jhola* etc.

For the weaving of silk clothes, women or the male members of a family, breed the silk worms on various plants. The silk *(Pat)* worm producing golden shining silk cloth are bred on the '*Nuni* Tree. Often these worms are grown on '*Champa*' or '*Mejankati*', Trees. After doing so, the silk worm weaves white '*Kova*'. As these silk worms of *Andi* are grown on *Era* or '*Raind*' plants that is how it got its name-andi. Eri is light brown in colour. Its weaving is attractive and long lasting. It is soft, light and warm.

If we pay attention towards the condition of women or men weaver, we will find that they seldom get the adequate returns of their labour. The liasoners or the middlemen purchase the clothes from these weavers at nominal rates and sell them with exorbitant profit into cities or other parts of the country. Houses without power looms, those people go and weave in somebody else's house on nominal wages or a salary of two meals a day.

[13] Tourist Places of Assam and Architecture

THE WORD - Assam plays a magical effect on the nature lovers. Famous for its natural beauty all over the world, tourists find Assam completely irresistible. Apart from the unparalleled scenic beauty the culture has a great diversity and variety as well. It is this diversity that has earned Assam the sobriquet of 'Little India'. One can find people from all parts of India inhabiting the state. This is why; Assam is unique and invaluable, not only naturally but also socially and culturally.

The best part about Assam is that the nature, which has prospered it with its youthful beauty, the same has provided the economical resources to the natives of Assam. The hilly deep forests of Assam are the storehouse of invaluable timber. Besides the availability of liquid Gold (Petroleum) is also the chief economical resource, provided by Nature.

The Tourists attraction towards the place and the resulting income due to Tourism is also a gift of the nature to Assam. Crux of the matter is that Assam & Eastern states have been bestowed with special blessings of Nature. Hence, the Love of music, beautiful natural simplicity and the assimilation of various communities, is the epicentre of Assam's glory & exquisiteness.

It has been mentioned in the previous chapters that Assam, that was known as Pragjyotishpur existed before

Tea garden

the Mahabharata period. Kalkipurana Yogin Tantra testifies this fact. It is believed that Maharaja Bhagdutta fought from the sides of 'Kauravas' during the war of Mahabharata. Several ancient places, memorials etc constructed by the ancient kingdom are being excavated and the same serves the reason of tourist's attraction, besides introducing the ancient culture & civilization. When we enter Assam's border from New Bogaiganv side by a train, we get the sight of the exceptional Natural grandeur of the place. However, as we hear about Kamakhya (a small station just before Guwahati) our body shivers with terror and curiosity. As the term "Kamakhya" reaches our minds through the route of Eyes, several uncertainties begin surrounding our psyche. The main reason is the spread of several deluding folk tales during ancient times. However, such issues are not prevalent now; but still having a human psyche one obviously feels curious. Therefore my mind pesters me to visit Kamakhya and I get desperate to reach there. From here onwards starts the Tourist program of Assam.

Guwahati

Ancient Pragjyotishpur is today's Guwahati. Pragjyotishpur was also known to be the capital of the ancient devil king Narkasur. Kind Bhagdutt had also ruled here. Even though there is no evidential reason about how the name Pragjyotishpur came into being, yet its meaning- "Ancient city of light" "(*Prachyaprakash Nagari*) seems quiet meaningful. The most famous Archaeologist Dr. Banikant Kakti, considering it as the set of few Austro Asian words, explains the meaning- as a state of huge mountains.

As we enter the Guwahati of today, significance of both the terms become obvious. Assam has been cited as the 'heaven' of Northeast India, where as Guwahati is termed as "Light of the East" according to which the name "Ancient city of light" (Prachyaprakash *nagari*) seems quiet reasonable. After having the sight of the Gigantic Neelanchal Mountains, the second meaning -States of huge mountains also seems reasonable.

Guwahati is known as the Gateway of North East India. Without reaching Guwahati one can't visit any of the Northeastern places. Guwahati is situated on the Banks of the Sacred River Brahmaputra. The scenic blue mountain series, which, along with the red colour of Brahmaputra, weave a unique and captivating spectacle around it. The only metropolitan city of Northeast India, encompassing the Natural beauty within itself, is situated along *'Lohit'*.

Guwahati is not only rich naturally, but also enriched with ancient art of architecture, forest life and natural civilization. Thanks to ancient historians and ancient evidences, Assam has also become a center for attraction in the field of Ancient art of *Vaastu*.

To reach Guwahati every Metro has the facility of airbuses. Besides, it is connected to all the corners of country by rail route. There is also the availability of regular air service between Delhi, Kolkata, and Guwahati. From the Guwahati airport services of Indian airlines & Vayudoot are available for Mumbai, Chennai.

There are several 5 Star, 3 Star Hotels & many modern Lodges & Tourist Bungalow's for Tourists.

Other places of attraction here are oil refineries, Museums & Zoo "*Dighli Pukhori* situated in the heart of the city is another tourist spot. The Kala Kshetra (art centre) of Shrimant Shankardev in Guwahati is also quiet scenic due to its magnificence, attracts a large number of tourists.

Kamakhya

Mother Goddess Kamakhya is widely known as *Kamru Kamaksha* (Kamrupa-Kamakhya). Ma Kamakhya's temple is 3 K.M away from the gateway of Assam Guwahati and is situated amidst the natural beauty of 700 feet high Neelanchal Mountain.

In fact Neelanchal Mountain and *Kamakhya Mahapeeth* are a exclusive confluence of splendour & meditation. Out of the 51 *Shakti Peeth's* mentioned in *Shastras*, Kamakhya in the most important. Though it is not mentioned in the *Devi Bhagvat,* but it has been praised in almost all the literature related to *Shakti Sadhna* (power meditation).

Shakti Peeth Kamakhya

Clouds on the mountains, forest foliage, melodic chirpings of different birds and the mystifying history- folk stories, the same Assam surrounded by temples, is known as the castle of curiosity & surprise.

This is a state of temples & *peeth* (benches). The most important *peeth* is "Kamakhya Peeth" the Centre of amazing & strange *siddhi* (salvation) of Tantra Mantras. This peeth is situated at a height of 600 feet. Neelanchal mountain jolts the tourist with the incredible beauty of this peeth, this might perhaps be the reason behind its immense popularity because the entire route to reach the peeth is exactly same as mentioned in the "*Vasantvarnan*" episode of Tulsi's "Ramayana". The scenic route, natural grandeur and the entire formalities of the temple awaken *adhyatma* (metaphysics) by digging it out. All the literature related to "Shastras, among the 51 Shaktipeeth, the Kamakhya shaktipeeth in the most important. It has been praised a lot in *Tantra Chudamani and Kunjika Tantra.* The entire saga of the origin of the universe, till its doom has been mentioned in *Tattva Chintan,* It is "Bhagvati" only who sit in this peeth, in the form of *Kamakhya* or *Mahamudra.* The meditators prefer this form of Bhagvati as shaktipeeth gives immediate results.

Several folk tales related to *Mahadevi* Kamakhya are prevalent. One of those is related to *Yajna* by Daksha Prajapati - The daughter of Daksha Prajapati- Sati was married to Lord Shankar. During one of the gatherings, Daksha Prajapati was annoyed with Lord Shankar over some issue. To avenge his insult he organized a *Yagya*, in that Sati and Lord Shankar were not invited when sati came to know about the Yagya she requested Lord Shankar to attend the *Yagya* Lord Shankar tried to convince her that it is not right to go any where without invitation Sati then decided to go alone when Lord Shankar denied her permission, she became angry. Finally, Lord Shankar had to give her permission to go to her father's place. When the father saw Sati in the yagya he reproached lord Shankar sati could not tolerate the abusing words against her husband. She gave up her life in the 'yagya kunda'. Furious with this incident *"Gana" (attendants)* of Lord Shankar destroyed the yagya and killed Prajapati. On Sati's mother's persistence lord brought Daksha back to life, but he could not free himself from the grief of Sati's demise the roamed around the world carrying sati's corpse. The whole world was in Chaus. Eventually, on the requests of *Devta* (Gods) Vishnu cut the corpse of sati in to pieces with his *Sudarshan Chakra.* Wherever the organs fell, a new shaktipeeth (holy place) originated.

The Assamese writer- Vishnu Rabha is of the opinion that "*ka-ma-kha*" or *Kamlakhi Devi* was the goddess of tribals of austrik group. Ka-ma-kha means "Sham shan dharini" or Goddess of ghosts and devils. Some people believe that "ka-me-kha" is the Goddess of Khasi (Meghalaya) tribes. It means Mother goddess.

There are several anecdotes associated with Kamakhya, one such is- Once Narkasur was attracted to Goddess Kamakhya and proposed her for marriage. Goddess put a condition that she would accept Narak's proposal if he gets the construction of the steps towards temple done in one night. Narkasur did all he could. When the steps were almost complete, the cock hooted, under goddess' influence. It was morning. Narkasur followed the cock & killed it. A little far from Kamakhya is *'Kukura Kata'* situated, where the cock was killed.

With time Kamkhya became the epicenter of 'Shaktipuja' (power worship) Many Meditators, Yogis got involved in Tantra Sadhana and the place became famous in whole of India as the area of Tantra Sadhna.

The Vaginal part of Bhagwati's organs fell on the

Neelanchal Mountain. Due to which it became blue. That is why it is called- Neelanchal and the "Peeth" on it came to be known as Kamakhya Peeth. There is a special meaning of the word Kamakhya, that is "eye of desire" because all the desire find an end at this place. Kamakhya is a form of "*Mahakali*".

At first the tourist take bath or wash themselves in the "*Saubhagya Kund*" and then go & offer prayers in front of Lord Ganesha's Idol in the nearby temple. Then greet Nandi Bhringi Idols at the outside of the temple and then enter. During Navratris tourists have to stand in row for around 3 to 4 hours before getting the "*Darshan*" (view) of the Devi. After entering into the temple, one gets the view of the Har Gauri Devi Idol situated in the middle of 12 pillars. After that one can see a particular idol made of 8 metals sitting on a throne. North to it are *Vrishvahana, Panchvaksha,* and *Kameshwar (Mahadev)* with 10 hands. To the south "*Vishishta Ashtavashlochna* "*Singhavahini,* Kameshwari or idol of *Shakti* sits on the lotus after her *darshana,* only the devotees can enter the Moolpeeth (It's a cave like *Garbhasthal (room with idol).* The solar lamps are always lit there.

The description of this place is important. In the 4 square mile area, on the upper side of the *Vishishth Shilapeeth,* water keeps oozing out from underground, Kamakhya's *Yonimandal* is located there. The total area of this Yonipeeth is one *hand* long, 12 *Angula* wide. It has *Sapulak Ashta hasta* and includes 50,000 *Pulkanvit Shivling.* Since it is a maternal organ, half of the portions is always kept covered with a Golden umbrella, However, some part of it is left open for worship, *Darshan* etc., it is believed that "Aadi Shakthi" When Pleased, is capable to provide the living beings both pleasure are Salvation means- *Moksha.* That is why this '*Mahapeetha*' enjoys an important position among all the Shaktipeeth. There is a custom of worship from south and left route. Saints and *sadhus* from all part of country come over here to worship or touch the holy water of the peeth.

After the 'puja' (worship) of 'mahapeeth' devotees worship the *Matangi*- Saraswati and *Kamala* or lakshmi peeth. As the devotees, come out of the temple, they see the idols of *'Bahudevs*, who represent prosperity' after this while chanting the Mantras go round the temple.

Apart from 'Bhagwati peeth' there are several other temples on the Neelanchal Mountain. Most of them are constructed with 'Tantrik' method lord. God Vishnu located near the temple has it own importance. Here Vishnu and Shiva are shown in a single idol, that is a great work of art. By any reason if a devotee is a unable to visit Shiva temple, he can take a "darshan" of Shiva of this temple to acquire the right of Bhagwati's Darshan. Along with 'Moolpeeth' and other Gods and Goddess' idols and temples, there are also *'Dus Mahavidya'* and *Panchvakya Mahadev* temples. There is an interesting story related to these *dus mahavidyas (ten).*

This place is well populated today. A small city seems to have settled there. There is a Sanskrit school. Arrangement of secondary or higher secondary education is there. Library, post office, police service, Government Hospitals are all available. From Guwahati till the peetha, one can walk down on foot and there is other route as well.

Regular bus service is available, till the temple. In comparison to Guwahati, the hill environment here is unsurpassed from the point of view of, health and scenery. The hill View becomes so attractive during winters that tourists tend to visit the place again and gain. The arrangement of lodging for the tourists is traditional that is in the houses of the *Pundits* here. However, the town being near and due to frequent bus service, tourists prefer to stay in Guwahati reason being unavailability of lodges or Tourists houses. Besides the scarcity of drinking water and electricity also take the tourists towards the city. In the congress session, Shri Govind Vallabh Pant (then Home minister) took the responsibility to construct road from the base to top and he completed the mission. Before this. This part was connected with the city with a footpath.

Umanand

It is located in the middle river Brahmaputra in Guwahati. There middle of it is one hill-shaped island in the middle of it -which is called Umanand. It is basically a Shiva temple. After the *Darshana* of this temple only, devotees can move towards Kamakhya temple -this is customary.

According to mythologies after Sati's demise, Shiva went under meditation on the Neelanchal Mountain. This had happened due to his immense love for Sati. He felt Sati here and he found happiness; that is how this place got its name -Umanand. People believe that due to his love for Sati, Shiva stays here. Kamdev was incarnated here, Because Shiva had so promised Rati. Thus, after the Darshan of Umanand tourists move toward Kamakhya Pilgrimage. The distance between Umanand and temple is about seven or eight km. One can see the majority of 'Pandas' here. In addition they register the names of the whole family of the tourist. If any of the relatives of the tourist had ever gone there before or if he had not gone, in any case one has to register ones name and address. Almost all the pilgrimages of India have such tradition. However unlike other pilgrimages the pandas of this place do not trouble the tourists.

Navgrah Temple

According to the mythologies Pragjyotishpur was famous as the bench of Astrology or related science. The adventurous stories of the "tantrapeeth" give goose bumps to the listeners. According to *'kalkipurana'* Brahma the creator at first created the constellation at this place itself. From this point of view too, Pragjyotishpur is aptly named. Whatever be, but the live example of the establishment of Navgrah temple and Tantra peeth in Kamarupa are the

Navgrah temple and Kamakhya temple and these are the main centers of attraction for the tourists coming here. Ancient Devil king Narkasur constructed Navgrah temple. Today's Guwahati city- Ancient Pragjyotishpur is also believed to be constructed by him.

The mind & eyes get desperate to seep in the whole of the scenic galore of the sunset in the hills of Bhuvaneshwari near Guwahati, when seen from Brahmaputra. Suddenly, when the city gets enlightened, it seems the heart is enlightened by same godly power.

Hajo

Around 14 km from Guwahati, Hajo, too is an important pilgrimage. It attract nearly all the tourist be it Hindu,

Hajo : A confluence of communal harmony

Muslim or Buddhist devotees towards itself. Near Guwahati, on the banks of river Brahmaputra, there is an Ashram of saint Vashisht, which refreshes the memory of ideal woman, when Ram threw out pregnant Sita from home. In the Middle of Guwahati city, there is an "*Ugratara*" temple situated on the Shukreshwar hill, also attracts a lots of tourist's attention. Janarden temple is also located here.

Haflong

Located 353 k.m away from Guwahati Haflong is very attractive and scenic hill place. It is the headquarter of north Kachchar district. It is the most adventurous hill center of Assam. One can always see rainbow in the valley down. The peaceful solitary atmosphere of this hilly region seems like the music of the prayer. The thunderous clouds seem like the playground of some carefree adolescent boys. The green horizon gives the thrill of some melodious tune. The sunshine of Haflong valley presents an unforgettable picture. The mountain area of Assam is quiet romantic and exciting. It would not be an exaggeration if we compare Assam with heaven. The mountain seem swimming in the

Halong Lake

sky.

Both road and rail transport are available to reach Haflong. Nearest railway station is lower Haflong. Tourist lodges, Government guesthouses and hotels are available for the tourist.

Nagoan

Nagoan is 123 k.m away from Guwahati. Bus service is available to reach here. Nagoan is not only unique in its Natural exquisiteness, the economic and culture resources are also in abundance. Around 14 k.m away is the Vaishnav saint Shankardev's Birthplace. The birth anniversary of the saint is celebrated here as *'fagua'* festival. The Chapavala waterfall, just 22 k.m away, is another tourist spot. Nagaon was the capital of king Barphukan. This place had been plundered several times by the Muslim invaders. That is why it has a historical value. Saubhagya Madhav, Dulal Madhav and Gopal Madhav are the three ancient temples. These are the focus of attention of archeologists. Ahom king Shiv singh constructed these temples.

Around 34 k.m from Nagaon is a place called Dabaaka; it is located to the south east of Nagaon. The Akash Ganga waterfall of this place is a popular picnic spot. In Dabaka one can easily find the ruins of ancient temples, ruins of lakshmi Vishnu idols lying scattered, which have a great value for the tourist and archeologists.

Darang

Mangaldoi is the headquarter of Darang district and Udalgudi is sub headquarter. The Northern portion of this district is quiet populated. Mangaldoi is traditionally related to the Darang Bridge constructed by the Ahom king Pratap Singh. On the other side of it are some of there educational institute, Government offices etc. Road transport is available for Darang from Guwahati.

Darang district is also known for the mutiny. In 1894, the villages had revolted against the British. Bhairav kund, a religious place is located 14 k.m from Darang Udalgudi headquarter. Udalgudi railway station is also located there. Bhairav kund is a Natural lake, created by Dhanshri and Rota rivers. It is surrounded by Amrigiri hills Traditionally this lake is associated with Pandavas. It is believed that the Pandavas had taken a bath here during their journey to heaven; it is an appealing point for both tourists & devotees. Udalgudi is around 32 KM away from Mangaldoi. The people of Bhutia community came here via the hill route. They had come for trade purposes. In order to achieve the best they had started organizing a big fare since 19th Century.

Dibrugarh

Dibrugarh is an advanced city of Assam. It is famous nationally as well as internationally for its tea Garden & oil refineries. It is also known for its Coalmines. Dibrugarh is suitably connected with roadways & airways as well. Besides it is also connected with the culture & education of Assam. The Dibrugarh medical college, Dibrugarh university and Dibrugarh all India radio, make it all the more important.

Tinsukia

Tinsukia holds historical importance. Matak king of this place fought bravely against the Burmese. Tinsukia is a railway junction. This district is a trade center of upper Assam. The ancient refinery of Assam, located in Digboi is around 94 k.m away from this place. It is connected both with road and railways. Dumduma, Hanspung, Hugrijan, Kharjan are famous for crude oil. These are several coalmines contributing to the economic growth of Assam. Coalmines are spread in Lidu, Bargalai, Tirap, Lekh Pani Nam dang etc. There are plywood factories in Tinsukia, Mukum and Margherita.

Sadia is a sub headquarters of Tinsukia. It used to be a beautiful city before. But due to the 1950 Earthquake, the city was destroyed. In ancient times this place was known as Kundil Nagar. In the ancient epics, one can find the mention of the love story of Kundil princess Rukmini and Shri Krishna.

Tejpur

Tejpur is a popular tourist place. It was known as Shonitpur in ancient times. According to Mahabharata, Shonitpur was the capital of Banasur. There had been a great war between Hari or Vishnu (Krishna) and Har or Shiva over the issue of Banasuri daughter Usha and Shri Krishna's grandson Anirudh.

Tejpur is located on the northern banks of Brahmaputra. The place encompasses the memories of ancient ruins and

The maingate of Da-Parbatia

also the picture- sque natural grandeur. When we set our eyes on the rich green valleys of the Himalayas, and also the tea gardens of the north, we feel like locking the gold like natural charm into our minds. The archeological ruins found here are the focal points of ancient civilization.

Tejpur has been first and foremost in the field of literature and art, not only in Assam but the whole of India. Several art lovers like- Shri Chandra Kumar Agrawal, Anand Agrawal, Dandi Kalita and others were born here. "Roop Kunwar" is the famous creation of Jyotiprasad Agarwal, which serves as a torchbearer of Assamese art, literature and culture. Shri Jyoti prasad Agrawal, a famous poet, artist, literature, dramatist film producer and a brave freedom fighter took birth in this sacred place. He raised his voiced against the British in 1942.

A little away from Tejpur is Da Parbatiya temple, which is famous for its historical value. It is a focus of attraction for the tourists as it serves as a unique specimen of ancient art of vaastu and Architecture. On the entrance of this temple two idols of Goddess Ganga or Yamuna are shown holding Garland in their hands, it presents a unique specimen of artistry. The entrance is adorned with various ornaments, which holds a great archeological value.

Agni Garh

Agnigarh attracts the attention of young lovers. The place refreshes the memories of the love story of Usha and Anirudha. It is believed that Usha stayed with Anirudha in the palace surrounded by fire. Today's Agnigarh is merely a hilltop, standing besides the bank of Brahmputra River. The scenic beauty of which instigates the spirits of the tourists. In addition, its exquisite grandeur even glorifies Brahmaputra and Tejpur.

Maha Bhairav Temple

It is also one of the famous tourists places. It is believed that Banasur constructed the temple, where in he himself

Mahabhairav temple

use to worship Mahakal Shiva. It is also a best specimen of ancient art of architecture in Assam. Other tourist spots of Tejpur are Padam pukhri, Hajara pukhari, Chol Park etc. Bhalukpung is an attractive picnic spot. It is 60 k.m away from Tejpur. It is located at the base Aka hills. Bhalukpung's

Padm Pukhari

Chol Park

forte is its hot water spring that is located in Tipi. The orchid garden of this palace is a unique and innocent natural gift. The Ahom leader constructed a bridge on river Brahmaputra, which also attracts a lots of tourist attraction, having witnessed two centuries, it still survives and stands

The Kalia Bhomora Bridge

erect on Brahmputra. A new bridge has recently been constructed at the same place, which is 3.05 k.m long.

Kaziranga National Park

It's the only national park of Assam. It holds international acclaim for its natural wealth, forest life, creatures and wild animals. The park occupies an area of around 82 km. It is about 100 km away from Tejpur. To reach here one has to cross over the bridge constructed by Kalia Bhomora Phukan.

This park is famous in the world for its single horned rhinos. More over other wild animals like tiger, cheetah, elephants, cobra, water buffaloes, wild cats, golden apes, cap apes, single horned deers, stags and other animals attracts tourist from all over the world. To visit these parks Assam Tourism department had constructed Tourist bungalows equipped with all modern facilities. '*Dak* bungalows' have also been made for the tourist. Circuit houses are also available. There are several hotels, which not only provide lodging facility but also provide conveyance for the tourists to travel around.

As one reaches Tejpur, getting in touch with the tourist information officer would solve the entire problems. Besides, a daily bus service from Guwahati is available for the tourists.

Shiv Sagar

It is yet another tourist spot. It has also been famous for its work of art. It had been the capital of Ahoms who ruled Assam for over 600 years. Ahom Empire ended only after the Britishers arrived. This city was named after 'Shiva' it also illustrates the story of the destruction of a powerful empire. The main center of attraction here is the two hundred years old Shivsagar Lake, which spreads in the area of 130 acre. The lake is located in the heart of the city. The level of the lake water is above the city level. There are three temples on the sides of the lake – Shiva Dol Vishnu

Shiva Dol

Dol, and Devi Dol Queen Madambika, wife of king Shiva singh constructed these temples in 1734. Shiva dol temple is the best among all the Shiva temples of India. It is 104 feet high, and 195 feet broad.

A dol

Shiv sagar is also the center of production of crude oil & tea.

Kareng ghar

Talghar

About six km beyond Shivsagar is the seven storeyed 'Karengghar' and 'Tala tal Ghar' This typical seven storeyed house has its three storeys under the ground (which is known as Tala tal Ghar) and the storeys above the ground are known as "Kareng Ghar" this was constructed by Ahom king Rudra Singh in 1696 – 1714. There were two tunnels; one was connected with Dekhon River and the other with Godhwal palace. East India Company later on closed these tunnels.

Rang Ghar

It is also a tourist spot. It is a two-storeyed egg shaped structure. From here, the Ahom rules would view the

Rang ghar

elephant fights. And would take the pleasure of watching other sports activities. It was constructed by king Pramatt Singh in 1744 – 1751.

Gadhgaon Palace

It was the main city constructed by Ahoms. Suklemung got it constructed in 1540. It is about 13 k.m east of Shiv sagar. After the old temple got destroyed, king Rajeshwer reconstructed the seven-storeyed new palace in 1762.

Jai Sagar Temple and Lake

Tourists frequently visit lake and temple. King Rudra Singh in memory of his mother had constructed the lake. This temple and lake are located 5 k.m away from Rangpur and have a Great tourist and archeological value. These are located 8 k.m beyond Shivsagar.

About 12 k.m away from Shivsagar, is a stone bridge over the Namdang river, which was made by the labourers from Bengal, is a special specimen of workmanship and it's a must-see for every tourist, today's national highway no 37 passes through the same bridge.

Similarly there are several tourist places around Shiv sagar like – Charaidav, 28 k.m away from Shivsagar, was known to be the chief capital of Ahoms. 'Sukafa' constructed it in 1253 AD. Same way, Ajanpeer Dargah is also an important tourist place. The Dargah is 22 k.m away from Shivsagar. Ajanpeer was the first Muslim Saint who wrote "Jikir" in the Assamese language. A big fare is organized on the day of the "*Urs.*" Other important place are Vaishnav satr, Muslim Dargah, memorials of Buddha and Shakti.

To reach Jorhat, airways are available from Shiv sagar. Railways reach you till Guwahati. The Roadways are the best option to reach Shivsagar. Simmalgudi is the railway station, which is situated 16 km away from Shivsagar.

Tourist lodges, circuit houses, *Dak* bungalows are available for the boarding purposes. It is better to contact tourist information officer to avail several tourist facilities, bookings etc.

All said and done, whether Assam holds any historical importance for tourists or not; there is no doubt about the fact that Assam is unsurpassable and unique, from the point of view of its natural beauty.

The picturesque locations, mountains, river Lohit, snow covered hills, forest riches, etc take our fancy, besides, the life style, culture and the civilization also fascinates us. *Bihu* dance of this place presents a polite glimpse of its society. Where as the expertise of the women on the weavers loom also fascinates the tourists. The unadulterated beauty, love for people and innocence of this place are amazing and etched in ones minds forever. Although the terrorist and the insurgents from Bangladesh are amalgamating the atmosphere, otherwise the mutual faith and unity amongst the natives is unbeatable.

Art of Vaastu

Researches of mythologies and several descriptions and stories reveal that Narkasur, Bhagdutta, Banasur, and other devil kings were leaders in the art of vaastu or masonry. Narkasur got the kamakhya road constructed, overnight. The Shonitpur king Banasur constructed the Agnigarh for his daughter Usha to reside. These anecdotes tell us that Assam had since ancient period been ahead in the field of

A copper statue of Goddess Durga

Sketch of a Goddess on a copper plate

building construction.

The ruins of historical period of Assam since fourth century have been found. No other antique remains have been found of the period before this. According to archaeology the period before fourth century is inept to make known any information on Assam.

From fourth century onwards the construction of temple, palaces, forts etc had started. The evidences are the prehistoric ruins of the same. No original building of those times (before Ahom rule) are found, rather some of their remains can still be located all around Assam.

The documents of antiquity and inscriptions available reveal that the period before Ahoms saw construction of God, goddess temples. There is a reference of Surya temple in the 109 chapter of "Markande purana". According to the details provided by Chinese traveller HuanTsang, there were hundreds of temples in Kamrupa. One of the Surendra Burman's write up reveals that he got a Guha temple constructed and established in it an idol of Shiva. There is a reference in the Tejpur copper inscription of Vanmal Dev, which says that the damaged Shiva temple was repaired during in the same period. During the reign of Ratnapal in Guwahati, there is a reference of temples having white tomb shaped crest- (Sheersh), with idols of Shambhu established in it.

In the Nagaon copper inscription of Vanmal Dev it is described that the king got buildings constructed in a row. These buildings had several rooms. These rooms were decorated with the artistry of sculpture and painting. However these buildings & temples could not resist the climate, earth & natural calamities of Assam during the vast span of time and thereby destroyed gradually.

The history of art of sculpture and Vaastu in Assam of the period before Ahoms was in dark. There is no evidential document or inscription available to this regard, but current archeological researches have revealed several evidences. Various such mediums prove that Assam's art of Vaastu and Sculpture was deeply associated with the North India's advanced art Style.

The description of the Guha Temple in Neelanchal inscription of Surendra Burman appears quite similar to that of Kamakhya temple. Later on a temple was constructed there. Several specimens of the art of Vaastu at end of the Gupta period have been found from here. Then in the Ahom era, the Koch king Nar Narayan and Ahom king got it renovated. This suggests that the present Kamakhya temple has passed several levels since fifth century to acquire its present shape.

There is one more specimen of ancient art of Vaastu in Assam that is the "Toran Dwar" constructed towards the end of Gupta period in Da parvatia of Tejpur. It is an exclusive specimen of Gupta age style of Vaastu.

Constructed on the two doors and a head beam, the lovely 'Toran' has two idols of Ganga & Jamuna holding garlands, at the lower end of each door. Two halos show, behind each of these idols, illustrating godly qualities. Pictures of two royal cranes are engraved near the two idols, bowed snake idols, engraved floral and plant patterns enhance the grandeur of head of the door. On the head beam are five *chandrashalas* and each has a god idols engraved on it. This 'Toran' door shows a resemblance with the Sculpture of Patliputra & Varanasi developed during 5th and 6th century.

Da parvatia Temples have been renovated by digging their foundation. This temple is made of bricks and is a complete *purnang* temple. All the features of a *Purnang* temple such as "*Garbha Grah" or Mani Koop Mandap*" and *Ardh Mandap* are present here.

From Majgaon of Tejpur, the ruins of a temple, constructed towards the end of Gupta Age have been found. The head beam found here has the diagram of four temples and four of the April-ventilators arranged in an order one after the other. In these ventilations, idols of Gods are shown in a sitting position. It is assumed that these temples are older than the Daparvatia temples. Besides on the Bamani hills of Tejpur, ruins of temples are found in succession.

During the excavations of Barganga in Nagan district, *Garbh grah & Manikupa Mandep & Mukh Mandep* of a complete temple have been unearthed. Assam state Archeological organization has unearthed foundations of nine temples from 'Na-nath-than' excavations. Assam state

Archeological museum's excavations on the Madan Kamdev hills, near Baihata Chariali, around 40 km from Guwahati have found ruins of fifteen temples. Primary archeological researches have revealed about twenty of such temples. These the artistic style of the ruins of idols of various Gods and goddesses and statues suggest that these temples were constructed around eleventh or twelfth centuries. The couple statues found from here can be compared to the Statues of Khajuraho in Madhya Pradesh. The artistic style and presentation of the statues of Madan Kamdev are reasonably similar to that of Khajuraho.

The ancient ruins scattered around the whole of Assam reveal that several temples at various places had been constructed at the same time. These temples were based in the names of Shiva, Vishnu, Surya, Shakti and other Gods and Goddesses. At several places, along with the idols of Brahma, Vishnu & Shiva on the same beam sun & other planet idols have also been engraved. It is thus assumed that the temples were constructed in the names of various Gods & Goddesses.

In Assam the records of Ancient temples were found in the following manner :-

1. Toran : (Entrance) constructed on the entrance route, a little away from the original temple.

2. *Mukhya Dwar* : Temple's entrance gate.

3. *Mandap or Nat Mandir* : An assembly room.

4. *Antaral or Pravesh Path* : Way or room through *Mandap* to *Garbhgrah.*

5. *Garbhgrah* or *Manikut* : Ruins of God's idols lived there. In the *Purnang* temple, all three- *Garbhgarh, Mandap & Ardh Mandap,* use to be there. These are found in Da parvatia, Bar Ganga, Gupteshwar, Kamakhya & Madan Kamdev.

'*Vimana*' is the '*Math*' (an abbey) found on the crest of the *Garbhagrah (cental room).* It resembles a human body. It has legs, thighs & a crest. The crest is assumed as center and the style of the building construction is named.

Different from the Vaastu style of various temples based on the local secrets; It has developed its own distinctive style.

There has not yet been found any Vimana of any antique temple of the period before Ahoms, in its original form. Some beautiful diagrams of the temples have been found engraved on the head beams. These resemble the Nagar style temples. Several organ tips used in the *Vimanas* of Madan Kamdev temple have been discovered. These were constructed in accordance with 'Mel-Shikhars'. The aforesaid discoveries serve as the evidence of the *Vimanas* of the temples constructed before the Ahom age. It can be easily assumed that the floor of the crest angles and the mid potion of the crest from all side use to be covered with the artistically engraved panels. In the other types of Crests apparent portion of the organs are shown. The Upper organs of the temple can be divided into four parts.

1. Leg or Base 2. Thighs or the body sphere 3. Shoulder or *Gandi* (border) 4. Crest or head

The Thighs or the Body sphere rises up from the Leg or base portion. The shoulder portion turns inwards after rising parallel a little towards the upper side. The head portion starts above the shoulders. The portion above the shoulder is called *Aamlak* (Shaped like *Anwla*) *Khol* or *Khopdi* is above the *Amlak* and *Kalash* is on the top of the *Khopdi*. But on the diagrams engraved on organ tops & head beams do not show the upper portions of *Amlaks*.

The age before Ahoms clearly indicates the artistic style Vaastu in Assam. It was the result of the several western styles flowing into the status during the large span of time. One style was brought upon by Gupta Hindu stream; those are indicated in the *Torans* of Da Parvatia, ruins of Majgaon and few of the idols of Majgaon. Evidences of the other styles are the monasteries spread from Orrisa to North India. These monasteries comprised of only *Garbhgraha* with crests and narrow ways to enter the same. These narrow lanes were known as *Antaral*.

Madan Kamdev : Mini Khajuraho

The Assam was cut off from the rest of the World till recently. It is during the 60s & 70s the attention of the people was diverted towards this state. That is the reason why the medieval age historical places of Assam have perpetually been ignored. One of such derelict heritage is Madan Kamdev.

Various sculptures in Madan Kamdev

In Assam, there is place – Baihata Chariali around 35 KM from Guwahati. After crossing over a patch of footpath, one can find the ruins of Madan Kamdev, scattered all over a secluded place.

Madan Kamdev is spread in the vast stretch of 500 Meter. Uma Maheshwar's embraced idols, carved on the stones of medieval temples can be seen here. The main statues among these are that of Sun's, Ganesha's and Vidhyadhar's.

Archeologists differ on the issue of when was & who constructed these temples. But among them the opinion of Dr. Pradeep Sharma, Asstt. Director, Archeological Directorate, and Assam seems logical and evidential. He says that possibly when Capt. Daltan has written about 15 temple ruins found around the famous Silsako Bridge (a historical bridge that was destroyed in the 1897 earthquake) in his Asian Society of Bengal (1855) Magazine, then it might necessarily be about Madan Kamdev.

Again, after a long time span, in 1943 and 1949 AD, the inspector of Primary education, Tarnikant Sharma, gave same important information regarding the historical facts about the area, in the Assam research society (1949) magazine. But till 1976, no research work had been carried upon towards this direction. Mean while the religious people of the villages took the previous statues away or hunters carried them from one place to another.

In 1977, archeological Directorate, of Assam took over the charge & responsibility of this area. They started the excavations of the statues under the supervision of Dr. Pradeep Sharma, this exploration mission, had unearthed several interesting & valuable facts. According to them, apart from the main temple, ruins of 12 temples have been excavated. By observing these temples & the idols engraved on the walls, one comes to the conclusion that these were constructed during 10th & 12th century. According to Dr. Sharma Kamrupa (Modern Assam) had the rule of Pala dynasty. Thus Ratnapal, Indrapal and Gopal were the kings who might have had some hands in the construction of these. They reinforce their stand by reasoning out that similar evidences have been found in Cambodia. Anyway, not even a single type of stone inscriptions have been found on the basis of which, some cognate conclusion could be drawn.

The art of vaastu portraying the candid expressions of sexual acts can be seen in Madan-Kamdev after Khajuraho in Madhya Pradesh. The poses of not only Madan (Uma) & Kamdev's (Maheshwar) embraced idols, expressing various sexual acts are there, but also the innate sexual acts among elephants, lion, man & animal can be seen in the sculptures on the walls of the temples.

Bhairav with six heads, four headed Shiva, Kalpavriksha, Sun various *Apsara*, Vishnu with 6 heads, Saraswati and various other statues of animals have been found from here.

In the year 1977, when the refurbishment process of this area started, the hill was surrounded by immense variety of forests, snakes- scorpions, and wild animals like tigers. Even still, deep forests hem the place, and one can come across savage tigers and deers on the adjacent hills. On the other hand, the melodic chirping of the birds make the environment so pleasant and the natural milieu, strewn all ovaries very alluring. Right below the Kamdev river madankuri flows in the east and towards the north ,just beneath the hill is a vast stretch of swampy land which has the chain of hills of Gopeshwar from the north to west and Natuar nacha and Sangsari in the east. There are a few puranic beliefs prevalent regarding Madan Kamdev. According to one of those-God Shiva in a spurt of fury, had burnt god of love- Kam or Madan, to cinders. Madan was reborn at this place. According to another belief Madan was reborn here and had indulged in sexual intercourse with Rati.

Other than Madan-Kamdev (the main temple), ruins of other huge and small temples are also scattered around it. After viewing the ruins it can be easily inferred that among all the temples of medieval period, existing in the Brahmaputra valley, Madan Kamdev had an incomparable structure and possessed unblemished beauty. According to the Architectural directorate, there still exist the possibility of excavation of the ruins of twelve more temples.

It is a pity that all the undertaking have taken place only by the Architectural department. Various sculptures have somehow been amassed and kept at one place. The unusual statues are kept with care in a small gallery. Even still many statues are lying under the open sky. In order to protect them from Sun, water and cold, these statues have not yet been provided any chemical coating.

Nevertheless, archeological department has laid out a plan for the beautification of forest along with Tourism department, which includes, cleaning of madankuri river and equip it with boating, and setting up of a sanctuary and a huge art gallery.

[14]
Extremism in Assam

GENERALLY, Assamese are believed to be people of a gentle disposition, but it is not so. When it comes to protection of their communal vanity, they do not hesitate to fight unto death. History stands witness to the many occasions when they had taken up arms to protect their culture and communal identity. The recent example of that was the Assam agitation of 1979, when students in large numbers waged a battle against Bangladeshi infiltrators. the agitation shrunk and split on ideological grounds in 1981-82 resulting in a crises that led to the birth of organizations such as the AGP (Assam Gana Parishad) and the ULFA (United liberation front of Assam).

The Birth of ULFA

This terrorist organization took birth during the early years of the Assam agitation (1979-85). Originated basically with the aim of ousting the Bangladesh infiltrators, but later on was joined with other such issues, which had been detrimental for Assam for several years. For instance, the issue of unemployment, which was troubling the young minds. A state rich in natural resources found itself overlooked by the centre. This was also one of the issues of the movement. At the same time they were worried about the security of the Assamese culture. These and such other issues got the creative support of the social mind set in the movement.

All Assam students union (AASU) and Assam Gana Parishad had started a nonviolent and democratic movement, which lead to an extensive dissatisfaction amongst the revolutionary youths. These young men wanted to achieve their aim in an armored fashion. Intending so, a particular group of students formed the ULFA organizations on 7th April 1979 at the historical 'Rangghar' located at Shiv Sagar.

In the beginning, the founder members of ULFA were selected from the All Assam student union (AASU) and Assam Jatiytavadi Yuva Chatra Parishad (AJAYUCHAP). During the Assam movement, these members had participated with full vigour; the two prominent among these were Suren Dihingya and Bhimkant Badhgohain. However, with time both went into the background, and the ULFA became the monopoly of Paresh Baruah alias Pavan Baruah, Arvind Rajkhova, Anoop Chetia (real name Golap Baruah), Pradeep Alias Jagannath Gogoi, Naren Deka Alias Heerakjyoti Mahant and Sidharth Phukan alias Sunil Nath.

The Political wing of the organization ULFA is being run under the Chairmanship of Arvind Rajkhova, and Paresh Baruah is the Chairman of the army squad. The armed squad was involved in the extortion of money and other operations. The political and social service activities were carried upon by the organization. On one hand they collected money and on the other, the organization of ULFA started the mission against the various social evils. Like the Ban on the sale of liquor, getting the corrupt officials, (taking bribes etc) arrested and punished and punishing the miscreants behaving inappropriately with females. From 1989, onwards it started such activities and gradually ULFA acquired the image of an angel in the Assamese society.

The Beginning of Terrorist activity

The Terrorist activities began when, with an intention

to start armed struggle, the State Bank of India situated in Namrup (upper Assam) was robbed of 5.20 Lakh, in 1982. However this robbery was taken as just another usual Bank robbery. Meanwhile, many of its Chief supporters and members became the victims of the violence in the election of 1983.

Getting no results out of the Assam movement, the members of ULFA made up their minds to fight a decisive war. For armed struggle they required military training. To fulfil this aim, the members of ULFA, on 10th May 1985 carried upon a robbery on an extensive scale. They looted the UCO Bank situated in Guwahati, of around 8 Lakh of rupees and in the same month about 200 or 300 young men were sent across the Burmese border for military training.

On 15th August 1985, after a treaty between the members and the Central Government, the organization became almost inert. However, as the time passed these revolutionary youths lost interest in the Assam Gana Parishad. Consecutively, they held a meeting on 6th March 1987 in which it was decided to punish, the culprits of the 1983, bloody elections, who were also held responsible for the sorry state of Assam. Simultaneously, they propagated the endeavours of social & cultural development and carried upon such jobs under the Banner of -*Assam Jatiya Unnayan Parishad.*

Open Exploitation of the traders and Tea Gardens

This Terrorist organization gradually strengthened its roots in the Assamese society by doing several social work such as road construction, impeding prostitution, advising against liquor addiction etc. From here began the exploitation of businessmen and tea gardens for fund extortion.

In 1988, ULFA kidnapped and later on killed the former president of Kamrup chamber of commerce Girdhari Lal Harlalka, after being denied of ransom money. This murder spread a wave of fear among the business community. And the fear took its toll when on 20th January 1990 the then president of Kamrup Chamber of Commerce Shankar Birmival was assassinated. Late Birmival had called upon a trade "*Bandh*" against the illegal extortion of money from the traders by ULFA where as ULFA had ordered against such activity.

Again on 9th April 1990 Industrialist Swarajpal's brother and Chairman of Assam Frontier Tea Surender Pal was assassinated in Tinsukia during day hours. After that a wave of terror spread in the ULFA predominant areas like Dibrugarh, Shivsagar, Dhemaji, Lakhimpur, Shonitpur, Mangaldoi, Nagaon Guwahati etc and the businessmen who had come from outside, began returning back to their respective states.

The AGP Government proved a failure in stopping the illegal activities of ULFA and besides, it was being alleged that they were encouraging the ULFA. Meanwhile the process of extortion of money from the traders of the state continued and the political murderers also went on. ULFA was mainly bent upon uprooting the congress leaders and its supporters. Around 30-40 Congress leaders had been victimized by the ULFA.

ULFA Supporters and workers had penetrated deep in the states administrative and police departments. So the police could not dare to do anything against them, which gradually lowered the confidence level of the policemen.

Meanwhile, on 15th July 1990, the members of ULFA kidnapped the G.M. of Guwahati refinery H.K.L Das, his son and driver; they demanded the release of three of their members in lieu of them. In no time, a deal was finalized between state Government and the ULFA and on 29th July 1990 all the three ULFA members, including a dreaded member Heerak Jyoti Mahant was released. On the same day, a bomb explosion assassinated S.P of Dibrugarh, Daulat Singh Negi. This incident had further detoriated the morale of the police force.

Meanwhile ULFA recruited several new members and thus re-enforced its strength. The magnitude of the power of ULFA could be assessed by the continuous failure of Government in stopping the incident of murders, kidnapping and extortion, and the parallel Government of ULFA was running successfully.

In the villages their roots were penetrating deeply. People were regarding them as the *Nyayaykarta (judges)* even the then Chief Minister Prafull Kumar Mahant also had accepted the "Robin hood Image" of ULFA.

During 1989 and 1991 the publicity secretary of ULFA Sidharth Phukan organized several press conferences to put across the School of thought of - secular social Independent Assam, , and reasoned out that Assam had always been independent. For instance when in 1826 Britain and Burma signed the treaty of Yandabu, that time Assam was not a part of India. For Independent Assam, armed struggle was made the medium. The general Assamese had always had diverse views over this issue.

Operation Bajrang against ULFA

The increasing terrorism and the futility of the AGP Government lead the Central Government to suspend the state Government and prevail presidents rule in 28th November 1990. Simultaneously, ULFA was declared a Banned organization and "operation Bajrang" was started against it.

The failure of this mission (from 28th November 1990 to 19th April 1991) can be assessed by the fact that not even a single top leader of ULFA was arrested during this long time span. Although Army destroyed almost all the Camps of ULFA, and also the network of communication system and around 3000 people were arrested, but army could not lay its hands on their top leaders. Eventually. Operation Bajrang was aborted in April and in June 1991 the soldiers were sent back to the Barracks.

Meanwhile ULFA declared ceasefire from its side and

let the election of the state be held peacefully during May 1991. Congress (I) Government was formed in the state and meanwhile on 30th June 1991, when Shri Saikia along with his 36 members took oath, same day around 14 officials from different parts of the state were kidnapped. Among those kidnapped were commissioner & Joint Secretary of Personal Department of Assam Government S.K. Tiwari, supply superintendent Ranjit Das, Oil & Natural gas commission's Deputy G.M Jorhat, Narendra Sharma, Chief Geologist Bholanath Jaiswal, Store and purchase, Deputy Manager Shiv Shankar Gupta, Executive Engineer- C.R. Mohanty, ONGC's Engineer- Keshav Pal, T.S Raju, B.P. Shrivastava and soviet Engineer Grishinchako Sargai.

Demand of the supporters

ULFA demanded release of all its members & supporters from the jails. Initially Shri Saikia Showed a soft approach by declaring to release all the ULFA members, who had no serious cases against them. But the demands of ULFA went on increasing and meanwhile the situation took an explosive turn after the murder of the three kidnapped officials – T.S. Raju, Sargai and B.P. Shrivastava. Instantaneously, on the midnight of 14th September Army was called and operation "Rhino" started.

Not to repeat the mistakes during "Operation Bajrang" in the operations Rhino, the Army was made aware of the Assamese culture and other things, which brought upon visible results.

Meanwhile, ULFA's General Secretary Golap Barua Alias Anoop Chetia and his wife Jauli Baruah, and other two ULFA Members were arrested in Calcutta. And from then onwards, important clues related to ULFA started revealing. And dreaded ULFA members started being arrested. The ULFA Deputy Commander Heerak Jyoti Mahant was killed in an encounter in Guwahati, whereas publicity secretary Sidharth Phukan and other Leaders were arrested. The only leaders left now were chief of ULFA Arvind Rajkhova and

Commander in Chief- Paresh Barua.

Declaration of Ceasefire

The organization of ULFA met severe damages due to operation Rhino that resulted one-sided declaration of Ceasefire by ULFA on 17th December 1991 They showed faith in Indian Constitution and agreed for the peace talks. The change in ULFA's attitude and congenial atmosphere for talks Lead Government to release some of their top leaders- Golap Baruah, Sidharth Phukan and others. In fact, after that, several other ULFA members surrendered, who came to be known as S ULFA (Surrender ULFA). But this too could not solve the matter. According to the 2000 report of Home Ministry of Government of India, these are few of the active members of ULFA- Arvind Rajkhova (Chairman) Paresh Baruah (Commander in Chief) Sash Choudhary (Foreign Secretary), Raju Baruah (Commander of Operation wing) Asanta Baghphukan and Pranati Deka (Senior Leader). According to the report, ULFA is predominantly active in the Nalbari, Nagaon, Jorhat, Dibrugarh, Rangia, Tinsukia and Guwahati regions. ULFA is deeply connected to ISI, LTTE, People liberation Army (PLA), National Democratic front of Bodoland, Bodo liberation tiger force and their camps are in Bangladesh, Haflong, Mauli Bazar besides Marshala, Sukmi, Dalim, Koypani and Orang in Bhutan.

If we look at the reasons of spread of ULFA in Assam the following facts

Surface : The easy movement of weapons and terrorist due to unguarded boundaries, administrative inactivity and corruption, the ramshackle police system under political and other pressures, penetration of ULFA supporters and informers in the administration and police department" and full support of Pak backed' ISI to the aforesaid organization.

The indifference towards the Villain of Assam - ULFA

When ULFA gave the slogan of "Independent Assam. It

impressed the people who belonged to the middle or higher class in the administration, universities. They were of the opinion that an organization should exist which can fight against the center. Apart from bureaucracy, a big group of Police and Intellectuals of society stood up behind ULFA. They helped the organization. The local media highlighted the issue of their activities so much, as if they were going to be a part of some revolution.

Initially ULFA, in its social and developmental endeavours, like banning of Liquor sale at several places, arresting the corrupt officials, helping in the construction of damaged roads & bridges, created the image of 'Robin Hood' in Assamese society. But they could not live up to this image for long. The continuous kidnappings, murders, ransoms, shattered the hopes of the general Assam Society. The peace loving Assamese masses could not appreciate all this. Newspapers wrote about the opulence and squandering of ULFA leaders and the fact that they have diverted from their original aim, became apparent. They limited their aim to merely extort money by threatening or killing.

For example, the killings of social worker Sanjay Gosh (1997), Dancer Rashmi Bora, and their Appeal not to participate in Kargil war, connection with foreign terrorist organization such as ISI, usual endless Bandhs, the Bomb explosion of New Jalpaiguri on 22 June, 1999, all these shook the peace loving general public of Assam. The Public started believing that all this is merely ruining the image of Assam and so the distance between the ULFA & Assamese society increased. And without the backing of the society, no movement or mission can sustain. Truly speaking, ULFA no more has any hold over Assamese society. In the year 2000, the killings of 110 workers of Bihar from October till December have shocked the Assamese society and in retaliation people have come out on streets. In the words of Homen Bargohain, editor of Assamese daily –Amaar Assam' - 'The brain of ULFA is actually a zero'. Can 2000 riflemen oppose 20,00000 strong Indian Army? Besides, which Independent Assam does he speak about? When Naga Extremists are demanding one third of its part. Other tribes are demanding separate lands for them and fighting amongst themselves. In fact ULFA itself is not clear about the boundaries of Assam. To top it ULFA does not enjoy the support of the masses thus ULFA is left to be a bunch of devious youths, whose leader or workers want to lead a lavish life with the help of money generated through abduction or extortion. It would be appropriate to call them useless, who are living on the hard earned money of people. I would also thank (?) those regional reporters and newspaper owners, who hyped the even the pettiest of the issues. To increase the readership of the newspaper they would sensationalize the news items and created a paper Tiger out of ULFA. Therefore now the time has come, when Assamese people, without caring about their lives should openly oppose this futile revolution, because this organization is counting its last breaths. They not only lack funds, but not even getting foreign support. Due to political reasons Bangladesh cannot supply them with arms. Although for fighting these extremists are using their land. That is why, two ULFA members, who were caught in Bangladesh were handed over to India, as Bangladesh government does not want to offend India. Northern Myanmaar- has more than a dozen Camps of terrorists groups. But there is no evidential indication that the government there is supporting the terrorist like the Pakistanis are supporting J & K Terrorist. The ULFA Camps are there in Bhutan, but they do not enjoy the support of Bhutaneese Government due to political reasons. That's why, a separatist movement cannot stand on its own feet and sustain the fight for a long time against a powerful India.

The agitation of ULFA weakened also because the aim with which it was constituted had an intrinsic sentiment that Assam had always been independent. Before British came, it had been independent for 600 years. Ahoms ruled from 1228 to 1838, even Mughals could not win over the Ahom state (ASSAM).

But during the formation of ULFA, its leaders forgot that they couldn't work like the other separatist organization of Northeast. Such circumstances are not prevalent in Assam. They do not have a nature to survive hardships. Unlike Nagas who can survives in Jungles for months together. ULFA people or even the natives of Assam cannot stay in Jungles for long. Some people of Assam might abuse Delhi, call it imperialist or there might be some who had been raising their voices against exploitation by Delhi. But the whole of Assamese society has always been connected with the Indian Main Stream and basic nature of the society is not separatist.

Demand of Separate Bodo Land & Terrorism

Among the natives of Assamese Bodos are in majority. There total population is over 42.96 Lakh. Historians believe that Bodo Tribes came from middle Asia in 500 B.C. to settle in the valley of Brahmaputra.

Again during 13th century, Ahóm insurgents, who had come from east, took over this area & ousted the Bodo Tribes to the plain areas. This struggle went on for 300 years. Eventually, these tribes settled in the northern plain areas of Brahmaputra Valley. Kokrajhar & Ubalguri districts have around 90 percent of Bodo population. Where as in Rangia, North Lakhimpur, Sadia, Barpeta, Darang, Nalbari and other places have these tribes in minority. Identified by their diverse languages, culture and attires. The people are now recognizing these tribes. Rest of India didn't know much about them, but when Bodo people, in tune with Assam Movement, with the demand of separate state started a movement in 1985-86, they came in contact with the area outside the state then people started taking interest in the Bodo people.

Demand of Bodoland is Vintage

Its not that Bodo people put across the demand of separate State for the first time during 80's rather their demand is quict old. In 1927, during the British rule, these people proposed for the separate state, for the First time. In Kachari (Bodo) youth conference, presented a proposal to Simon commission, for their independent identity and demanded establishment of a separate Kachari regiment.

After the Independent of the country, the Northeastern hill tribes efficiently got their demands fulfilled. This is the reason behind the formation of Nagaland & Mijoram state in 1962 & 1972 respectively. New status like Meghalaya & Arunachal Pradesh came into being but in this race the tribes of the plain areas lagged behind; the Bodo's were the Chief Tribes among them.

Economical Backwardness : Main problem

In fact the main problem of Bodo Tribes is their social, economical backwardness. Official information reveals that 70 percent of the tribes are landless. Where as 90 percent of the tribes are dependent mainly upon ?. Outsiders had been dominating over the lands of these tribes, for many years. During 90's the AGP Government accepted that around 2.5 Lakh *acre* of Land had been illegally occupied by outsiders. To Solve Bodo Problem, center intervened and called up a meeting for tripartite talks in August 1989. But nothing came out of this meeting. Similarly many meeting were held during Janta Dal Government.

Bodo tribes in order to Secure the vanity put more focus on the demand of separate state and for this in 1967, all Bodo students Union (ABSU) and a political Party – Assam plain tribal council (PTCA) was formed; which split later on. But the demand of separate state did not end. The intensity of Bodo movement can be assessed by the fact that its form was run on the similar lines as those of the movements of - All Assam students union and Assam Gan Sangram Parishad, from 1979 –1985.

After the "Assam treaty in 1985, when the young leaders sat on Dispur seat they had to - the face troubles. The plan of ousting the foreigners had not yet materialized, when the AGP Government was shocked with the Bodo movement, That is why, then Chief Minister had to call upon the army in March 1989 after having seen their aggressive attitude.

At that time the young Bodo terrorists would burn the houses, would suddenly attack & snatch the weapon of Security forces, these incidents worsened the situation. Non-Assamese started fleeing from Bodo areas. Situation took a dangerous turn, when Bodo Terrorist targeted government employees. Due to the constants Bandhs, during that time the social life went into Chaos. Blasting of train tracks and trains and other such incidents introduced the aggressive attitude of the militants.

Moves in the Pretext of Movement

Bodo agitation proposed 92 demands across government. The main demands were a) Separate state Bodoland, to the North of Brahmaputra b) To the South of Brahmputra, new Independent district of the tribal areas c) To include Bodo Kachharis & other tribes of Karbi Anglong in the 6th Clause of the constitution d) To grant reservation facility tò maximum no of Bodo's e) To include Bodo language in the 8th Clause.

Then Chief Minister Prafull K. Mahant and Home Minister Bhrigukumar Phukan, refused the demand of separate State of Bodo people & said that the social and economic demands of the Bodo people can be met but the further division of Assam would not take place in any case. On the context of these demands Shri Mahant and Phukan called upon a meeting with Bodo leaders, which proved to be fruitless.

In the pretext of the movement, the backdrop of Political moves, began to form and the ruling AGP alleged Congress (I) of encouraging the Bodo Terrorists.

The social welfare minister of Assam Ms. Rekha Rani Das, alleged the Central State Minister, Mohandev that he had a secret treaty with ABSU Leaders. Meanwhile, many Bodo Leaders started saying openly that the solutions of the problem lies only in the armed revolution. N Hajri of ABSU formed "Armed Bodo Security Force" in order to save Bodo Tribes from the dual Polices of AGP & its Leaders. A training Camp was opened in the deep forests of Bhutan to train the Bodo terrorists, and a underground gun factory was also established there.

After the Bodo agitation took such an aggressive stand, Mahant Government called the Bodo leaders for talks on 28 February 1989. But they were bent upon their demands of a separate state and they agreed to come only if it was met. Therefore, the meeting failed. After the failure of this idea, state Home Minister Bhrigukumar Phukan wrote a strong letter to the Central Government that they have their direct involvement in the entire movement.

After blaming on to the Central Government, AGP Government ordered stern actions against ABSU terrorists, which forced several top Bodo Leaders to flee towards Meghalaya, West Bengal and Myanmaar. Shri Phukan said that demand of a separate state is invalid because the population of Bodo tribes in the Kokrajhar District was just 27 percent.

Meanwhile, Bodo people alleged torture by the Police. Incidents of their homes being burnt & rapes came into limelight, on the other hand, enforcement of Assamese language & Culture made the Bodo insecure about the existence of their own language & culture. Where as, Shri Phukan believed that natives of Brahmputra Valley are all outsiders no one is originally tribal. Therefore, all the people of Assam are Assamese. As the pressure from AGP increased, the Bodo movement became more & more aggressive and people started considering AGP as the party of particular Hindu Group. After the sudden death of President of ABSU Upendra Nath Brahm, in 1990 it seemed that the movement would now become directionless. But immediately, S.K. Bishvamutyari was made the President. He kept the pressure tactics, over the centre and State Government and propagated the movement. This resulted into the formation of 3 member committee under the President ship of Bhupender Singh (13 September 1990) to solve the Bodo problem.

Suggestion of greater Independence :- The aforesaid expert committee had to submit its report on 31st December 1991. But due to late census in Assam report too got delayed. Again a tripartite meeting was held on 7th January 92, but it too didn't lead to any satisfactory results. Now situation there is that a new organization National democratic front of Bodoland (NDFB) and Bodoland Liberation Tiger (BLT) are frequently raising their Voices to demand separate state. And thereby they are destroying the peace of the state with their violent activities. They are killing innocent people in the violence such as blasts in trains & buses. Not only this, the houses of non-tribal people are being burnt and they are threatened & forced to leave the area.

The Karbi Anglang Movement & Terrorism

Apart from ULFA & Bodo problems, the demand of Karbi Anglangs for independent state is also one of the serious problems of the state. Several tribes are struggling for their social cultures, economic & Political rights after being suppressed or ruled by non-tribal or elite Assamese community, after eventual dissatisfaction that resulted out of their ruling.

In the North Kachar & Karbi Anglang Hill areas, people are demanding separate state for last 15 years.

There basis of demands is not new. In 1969, when Assam reconstruction Bill was passed, the Mikir Tribes and the hills of North Kachchar linked with the Garo, Khasi, Jayantia were not merged with Meghalaya on the assurance of making them independent districts. However, they were given the option to get included within Meghalaya. Under this arrangement two independent district boards were formed under the 244 (a) clause of constitution, an option was given to the people that whenever they desired an independent State shall be formed. On this basis ASDC is pressurizing to convert these districts into an independent state.

The people demanding independent state allege that Assam Government has not paid adequate attention towards the development of Karbi Anglang. Instead Congress (I) and AGP Government Started intervening directly into district Board. Even after being autonomous the Budget of the district is made by Assam Government In the Recruitment of Employees, and other developmental places, the district Board does not enjoy any constitutional rights. Under such condition the dissatisfaction among the people of the district is natural.

Autonomous State demand Committee (ASDC) has been ruling for many years. It is surprising fact that a ruling party was involved in a movement. The leaders of ASDC had fully supported the "Assam Movement." With a treaty with Rajeev Gandhi Government in 15th August 1985 this movement ended. Although ASDC has to its possession the office of the district Board at Difu since 23rd January 1989, But it has not called off the movement. Meanwhile ASDC has been severely alleged.

The incidents of Kidnapping, Ransom, murders in Karbi Anglang still continues to happen. Karbi Volunteer force (KVF) is demanding a separate State. Other terrorists Groups of Karbi Anglang are Karbi National Volunteer (KNV) and United Peoples Democratic solidarity (UPDS).

In short we can say, Assam has same no of terrorists group as are its tribes state. And each group is demanding a separate state. And to achieve this they don't even hesitate to kidnap or kill. Few of similar terrorists groups are – Rabha National Security force (RNSF) Dimasa Halong Daoga (DHD) Muslim Liberation Tigers of Assam (MULTA), Kamtapur

Liberation organization (KLO) & Koch Rajvanshi security force (KRSF) etc.

ULFA & NDFB are banned in Assam and their activities are declared illegal. But the scenario is a Petty person would extort money in the names of these groups. The security scenario is, 13 Indian securities Battalion are posted in the Northeast. In Assam alone four Battalion are posted. For these battalions Central Government spends 50 percent whereas 50 percent is met by long-term interest free loan granted to the state Government

Center Granted 73.15 Crores for security arrangements, in the year 2000-2001. Similarly for security related expenditure in Assam, 258.84 crore was granted in 1997-2000. But still the formation new groups continue. Actually there is some social & economical reason too, attached with the terrorism or separatism.

As a matter of fact, the fund allotted for development of State by the centre or state gets distributed among corrupt bureaucracy and only a little part of it is issued for development. There are several villages and areas till date, which are still remote, lacking in proper mode of conveyance. The people are so poor that they are forced to survive on fruits, fishes and river water.

Tourist Guide

Shankardev : Art Center (Kala Chhetra)

Place	Distance from Guwhati (in Km)	IMPORTANCE
1. Guwahati	—	Guwahati is the Gateway to India's Northeast. Guwahati literally means betel nut Market. In fact two words-Guwa meaning betel nut and Hati meaning a market form the word Guwahati. The betel nut trees

are found in abundance here. Guwahati is the only metropolitan city of Assam. The religious places and tourist spots of Guwahati include Kamakhya temple, Umanand, Navgarh temple, Bhuvneshwar temple, Gandhi Mandip (9 km away) Local science Museum, planetarium Triupati Balaji temple, Shankardev Kala Chhetra, Madan Kamdev (45 KM).

Vashist Ashram : Located at a distance of a kilometre from Guwahati railway station, the highlights of the ashram include an artistic temple, hall and a magnificent swing. The Ashram also has a stone inscription of Vashist Muni's wife Arundhati. Another pleasing site is Vashisht Ganga. A rapid waterfall that flows close to the ashram.

National Zoo : Around 5 KM away from the railway station is the state zoo and botanical Garden. There is a high tower inside the Zoo from were one can water the whole of Guwahati city. The zoo has large collection of animals and birds.

Museum : Close to the railway station, adjacent to 'Ravindra

		Bhawan' is the Assam State Museum. Here one can view the ancient and historical artefacts. The museum has a lake and a park in its frontage.
		Refinery : Guwahati Oil Refinery is known for its petroleum products. Refinery is at a distance 4 km from the railway station and has good lodging facility.
2. Sualkuchi	32km	The place is known for the regional handicraft. Assamese silk, clothes made of red stone, saries and other utility products attract tourist's attention due to their remarkable weaving style.
3. Hajo	32 KM	This place is known for its archeology and architecture. It is an amazing meeting ground for Hindu, Buddhist, and Muslim religion. Buddha temple and his idols seem to be nurturing secular feelings
4. Chondubi	64 KM	Natural lake and picnic spot. One can enjoy fishing and boating at this place
5. Bhairav Kund	137 KM	Located at the Border of Arunachal Pradesh and Bhutan, is an attractive picnic spot.
6. Darang	100 KM	Famous for winter carnival which is held annually

7. **Batdrava**	134 KM	Birthplace of shrimant Shankardev
8. **Barpeta**	137 KM	Birthplace of Vaishnav saint Shri Madhavdev
9. **Tejpur**	181 KM	This place is famous for the ancient architecture, vaastukala, and ruins of ancient temples
10. **Bhalukpung**	250 KM	Famous for it's natural beauty. Famous for picnic spots and various water sports
11. **Shivsagar**		Center of historical importance. It was the capital of Ahoms kings of medieval period; One can get the sight of various tea gardens.
12. **Haflong**	355 KM	The only hill station of Assam. The place is unparalleled as regards it's amazing and excuisite beauty which unwittingly touches the hearts of the tourists, enroute their eyes.
13. **Jatinga**	364 KM	This place is near Haflong. A place of various colorful birds. During night a particular species of birds would get attracted to the flame of a torch and perish after getting burnt.
14. **Kaziranga**	217 KM	It is the only National park of Assam. The single horned rhino of the place is famous world over. Birthplace of pelican. The other animals found here are

		tiger, elephant, lion, dear, wild duck, cobra etc. the best time to visit this park is between November till April. Tourist lodges forest departing lodges, dak bungalows, etc. are available. Bus transports are available to reach this place from Guwahati
15. Manas	176 KM	This place is known especially for tigers. Besides, elephants, wild cows and bulls, dears, hornvills are also found at this place.
16. Majuli	326 KM	The biggest river island in the world. The place represents Vaishnav civilization. Various satra stand erected enclosing Assam's culture, music, art, dances and plays. It is the habitat of colourful birds of diverse kind.
17. Pabitra	65 KM	This place is famous for. Center for conservation of wild species. The place is a home of animal species like tiger, cheetah, single horned rhinos, and also a variety of birds.

Index

F

G

H

I

J

K